Festival ANNUAL 10

Independents United

festivalannual.com
myspace.com/festivalannual
facebook.com/festivalannual
twitter.com/festivalannual

Festival Annual 2010

Editors: Josh Jones & Frank Lampen

Art direction & design: Rob Jones

Festival Annual logo designed by Brand42 | brand42.co.uk

Cover photograph: Victor Frankowski (paddling pool) or Monika Magiera (picnic area)

ISBN: 978-0-9563022-1-2
A CIP Catalogue record for this book is available from the British Library.

Conceived, created and published by
Independents United Ltd
Circus House, 5th Floor, 21 Great Titchfield Street, London W1W 8BA
Tel: +44 (0) 20 7748 5208
iu-hq.com

Printed and bound in Somerset by Butler Tanner and Dennis Ltd on FSC certified papers.

Isle of Wight 8

Download 22

RockNess 38

Glastonbury 54

T in the Park 86

Oxegen 102

Lounge On The Farm 106

Latitude 108

Lovebox 124

Secret Garden Party 136

Global Gathering 152

Camp Bestival 156

Sonisphere 170

Field Day 176

Underage Festival 178

The Big Chill 182

Standon Calling 196

Vintage at Goodwood 204

Boomtown Fair 206

V Weston 212

V Chelmsford 224

Leeds 232

Reading 248

Shambala 268

L.E.D Festival 272

Creamfields 274

South West Four 282

Electric Picnic 284

Bestival 288

This book was created by:

in association with 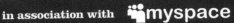 myspace

Aaron Twinky-Dj Williams, Aaron Wilson, Abbie Baxter, **Abbie Baxter**, Abbie Page, Abi Kennedy, **Abi Turner**, Abigail Lucy Hutchings, **Adam 'Curry' Rees-Murray, Adam Carr,** Adam Davis, **Adam Greenhalgh, Adam Gunn,** Adam Heyes, **Adam Humes, Adam Kettle,** Adam Klee, **Adam Phythian, Adam Postlethwaite,** Adam Searle, **Adam Sopp, Adam Starkey, Adam Tatton-Reid, Adam Toulmin, Aden 'Shakespeare' Beckitt,** Adrian Elliott, **Aidan Astle, Ailín Ó Conchobhair,** Aimee Brown, **Aimee Furnival, Aisling Bruce,** Aisling McElvaney Barbour, **AKI, Alan Hercher,** Alan Mackenzie, **Alan Morton, Alana Mustill,** Alasdair Fagan, **Alastair Moloney, Aleksandra Sladek,** Alex Agar, **Alex Bubba Bournat, Alex Ehmcke,** Alex Eveson, **Alex Field, Alex Gabrysch,** Alex Guppy Griffith **, Alex Hayes, Alex Kaylor,** Alex Kimbrough, **Alex Loughlin, Alex Louise Riding,** Alex Magicman Kasam-Sharples, **Alex McCormack, Alex Mellowship,** Alex Richmond, **Alex Rush, Alex Saunders,** Alex Somogyi, **Alex Strachan, Alexandra Hédreul,** Alfie Miller, **Alfonso Muñoz Sahr Staley, Ali Mcquillan,** Ali Moore, **Alice Hill, Alice Hunter,** Alice Pape, **Alice Shearon, Alice Windsor,** Alina Mingham, **Alisha Walklate, Alison Forsyth, Alison Malcolm, Alison Veal, Aliss Higham,** Alistair Heath, **Alixandra Lord, Allison Pinglaux,** Alun Owen, **Amanda Brazendale, Amanda Brown,** Amanda Clarke, **Amanda Dunbar, Amanda Green,** Amanda Rodaway, **Amber Starrs, Ammelia Phillipa Bryany Wells,** Amy 'Rusty' Ruston, **Amy Carsen, Amy Gillard,** Amy Gold, **Amy Greatbatch, Amy Langston,** Amy Lingard, **Amy Lodge Earnshaw, Amy Niven,** Amy Russell **, Amy Swift, Ana Goncalves,** Andrea Innocenti, **Andreas Armstrong, Andrew 'Mogley' Rose,** Andrew Blair, **Andrew Bradford, Andrew Dewey,** Andrew Gould, **Andrew Hickling, Andrew Joy,** Andrew Naylor, **Andy Boyd, Andy Brooks,** Andy Crow, **Andy Davies, Andy Davis,** Andy Horle, **Andy Jones, Andy Lock,** Andy McCormick, **Andy Moloney, Andy Richard Wilde,** Andy Routledge, **Andy Storr, Aneurin Bevan,** Angel Marie Roberts, **Angela Campbell, Angela Wright,** Angie Wilson, **Anita Stevenson, Anna Hudson,** Anna Hyams, **Anna Mansell, Annabelle Honess Roe,** Annabelle Pipparelli, **Annie Wright, Ant Nicholson,** Anthony Harper, **Anthony Riley, Antony Delahunt,** Aphra Kadabra, **April 'Drakers' Drake, Archie David Smith,** Ash Sweet, **Ashleigh Targett, Ashley Coates,** Aunty Joe Joe, **Aymen Ahmed, Barry Chambers,** Barty Mee, **Baza Anglais, Becca Darwent-Black,** Becky Beynon-Lewis, **Becky Heaton,** Becky Matthews, Becky Notley, **Becky Unyolo, Becky Wright,** Bekki Cook, **Bekki Stead, Ben,** Ben Carroll, **Ben Fullerton, Ben Gavin,** Ben Helsby, **Ben Hosie, Ben Jackson,** Ben McCarthy, **Ben Mills, Ben Murphy,** Ben Sullivan, **Ben Swinney, Ben Tj Campbell,** Benito 'Perromuchacho' Camela, **Benjamin Jones, Benjamin King,** Benjamin William Redway Redford, **Benni Coates, Beren Fryer, Bernie Kennedy, Beth Camilleri,** Beth Durant, **Beth Hooper, Beth Roberts,** Beth Williams, **Beth Wright, Bethan Hamer,** Bethany Jones, **Beverley Moffitt, Bex Watson,** Bill Marney, **Billy 'Danny' Murphy, Billy Bob Jackson,** Bobbie Anna Mellor, **Bobby Doyle, Braby Alexandra,** Brandon Egley, **Brannon Hall, Bree Cullen,** Brendan Greenfield, **Briony Latter, Bruce McArthur,** Bruce Salter, **Bryony McEwan, Bryony Thiedeman,** Buttfairy, **Caitlin Baird, Caitlin Naomi Morris,** Caitlin Shepherd, **Callum Owen, Camilla Pie-Face Smart,** Carina Millis, **Carl Cook, Carl Jones,** Carlene Natasha, **Carmela Tucker, Carol Calamity Quinn,** Caroline Bardon, **Caroline McCall, Carrie Quantick,** Cat Eagles, **Cat Grief, Cat**

Moss, Cat Sparkle Sparkle Mercer, **Catherine Ward, Cathy Minto,** Catia Riva, **Catriona Lyons, Catriona Quinn,** Caz Brooks, **Celine Haddad, Ceri Peplow,** Ceri Smith, **Cesca Barry, Cessi Wan,** Chantal Ward, **Charlee Drummond, Charley Garbett,** Charlie Cactie Cooper, **Charlie Delahunt, Charlie Errington,** Charlie Hewitt, **Charlie Hollinshead, Charlie Miller,** Charlie Mower, **Charlotte Branscombe, Charlotte Eastwood,** Charlotte ElectroFudge Fitzgibbon, **Charlotte Merricks-Mulligan, Charlotte Millbank,** Charlotte Rogers, **Charlotte Woods,** Chelsea Waterman, Chelsie Rogers, **Chen Ryan, Cheryl Ballantine,** Chev Donaldson, **Chirag Gupta,** Chloe Elkin, Chloe Haywood, **Chloe J Pickstock, Chloe Matthews,** Chloe Stevens, **Chris 'Baggy' Baggett, Chris 'Chezney' Burgin,** Chris Aaron Hall Murch, **Chris Charleston, Chris Clark,** Chris Cowley, **Chris Currie, Chris Everitt,** Chris Fittes, **Chris J P Franks, Chris Lewtas,** Chris McGuinn, **Chris Morgan, Chris Morrison,** Chris Raggy Ashley, **Chris Sanderson, Chris Scott,** Chris Sheils, **Chris Tinkler, Chris Wragg,** Chrissy Styles, **Christine Stewart, Christopher Purnell,** Christopher Thomas, **Christy Romer, Ciara Turner,** Cici Cavanagh, **CJ Stanley, Claire Baker,** Claire Booth, **Claire Brush, Claire Catling,** Claire Harvey, **Claire Louise Turner, Claire Muge,** Claire Paul, Claire Raby, **Claire Rennie, Claire Sprouting,** Claire Thompson, **Claire Tulloch, Clare Burrows,** Clare Cooney, **Clare Sutton, Colin French,** Connaugh Marie Fallon, **Courtney Armstrong-Clark, Courtney Platypus Armstrong-Clark,** Craig 'Barra Lad' Phillipson, **Craig Cragga Busby, Craig Crumbs Stewart,** Craig Dean, **Craig Denton, Craig Donkin,** Craig Easton, **Craig Garbett, Craig Lloyd-Jones,** Craig Thomas, **Cristina Avadanei, Cyan Fullbrook,** Cyrielle Henry, **Daisy DIY, Daisy Golding,** Daisy Lewis, **Daisy Negus, Dale Lemans,** Dalia Darko, **Dan Bam,** Dan Boydon, Dan Hubble, **Dan Jukes, Dan LeFro Gleeballs,** Dan MigraineSpank Bond, **Dan Prescott, Dan Sumners,** Dan Timmins, **Daniel 'Cookie' Cooke, Daniel Anderson,** Daniel Cunningham, **Daniel Hawkins, Daniel Hills,** Daniel Linter, **Daniel Saddington, Daniel Whitfield,** Danielle Gourlay, **Danielle Harvey, Danielle Louisa Robinson,** Danielle Mullins, **Danielle-Marie Fawcett, Danny 'Seymour' Tomlinson,** Danny Booth, **Danny Liu, Danny Walker,** Darren Vibert, **Dave Aslett, Dave Lee,** Dave Merrilees-Kelly, **Dave Redscale Beveridge, Dave Spedding,** David Beckett, **David Dunbar, David Gibbons,** David Hall, **David Hockster Hopkins,** David Ko, David Michael Bellamy, **David Sanderson, Dawn Halpin,** Deage Paxton, **Dean Houghton, Dean Kay-Barry,** Dean Williamson, **Debbie Darlington, Debbie James,** Deboradh Nolan, **Declan Holbem, Demelza Kingsland,** Denis O'Hare, **Di Jones, Dick,** Dod Morrison, **Dom Moore, Dom Moore,** Dom Taylor, **Dom Williams, Dom Wolfe,** Dominic Dennis Pagan, **Dominic Wells-Cole, Don 'Pablo Rojo' Remlett,** Drew Gibson, **Dylan Bayliss, EASTROAD,** Echolise Nicole Sutherland, **Ed Thomas, Eddger Emmanuel Beckford II,** Eddie Feltham, **Eddie James, Eddy-Cobra Team-Stone,** Eilidh Nelson, **Eleanor Cranfield, Elias Comnenos,** Elisabeth Bond, **Elizabeth Matthews, Elizabeth Ophelia Alice Rose,** Ella Aiken, **Elle Hardwick, Elleisha Adriana,** Ellen Ball, **Ellie Cunningham, Ellie Hopkins,** Ellie Liddell-Crewe, **Ellie Morgan, Ellie Wells,** Ellie-Jay Harrison, **Elliot 'Elski' Whiteside, Elliot Irving,** Elliot Mills, **Elliot Muharrem, Elly W,** Emanuelle Sangster, **Emer Herron, Emer Herron,** Emi Matsui, **Emily Abbit, Emily Brown,** Emily Elizabeth Woodhouse, **Emily J Hollands, Emma Chamberlain,** Emma Gardner, **Emma Harrison, Emma Huelin,** Emma Purvis,

Emma Rhodes, Emma Storey, Emma Vaughan, Enirak Siragluov, entwined Rose Songs, Eoin Crotty, Eoin Hanlon, Erika Patterson, Erin O'Brien, Erling McCracken, Euan Simpson, Eugene Tighe, Eunan Anderson, Eva Willsher, Evan Fleetwood, Fay Woodford, Faye Elizabeth Bradbury, Faye Harrison, Fedde Fresco, Felipe Leal-Adrades, Ffion Jones, Fi Foster, Flamey Hairwild, 'Flannol' Rosa, Flo Bayliss, Fran DeVille, Fran Hale, Francesca Harris, Frankie Mann, Franky 'Downs' Coleman, Freddie Churchill, Freddie Fennessy, Freddie Smithson, Freddy Stevens, Freya Efes Isin, Fumina Okamura, Gabe Cole, Ganesha Lockhart, Gareth Price, Gareth Rhys, Gary Allan, Gary Smear-Test Brown, Gary Stinton, Gary Windows, Gavin Bailey, Gavin Iamarealreverend Thompson, Gelli Graham, Gemma Ketley, Gemma Lewis, Gemma Norman, Gemma Paine, Gemma Pharo, Gemma Sloggie, Geoff Bannister, Geoffrey O'Callaghan, George Blueb Ford, George Hayes, George Osborne, Georgette Crush, Georgia Moore, Georgia Strawson, Georgie Wilson, Georgina Tyson, Gheorghe Hemsley, Gill Shorty Morrison, Glenn Quartermaine, Go Outdoors, Grace Beech, Grace Maleedy, Grace Mercoo She'o Collas, Grace Naylor, Grace Rake, Grace Sofia, Graeme Fraser, Graeme Grove, Greg Franck, Grinnerz Minnerz, Guy Hilton, Hangtime Horner, Hannah 'Bing' Ingram, Hannah Crocker Dile, Hannah Davies, Hannah Ga Ga Graham, Hannah Kelly, Hannah Lanfear, Hannah Le Masurier, Hannah Loukaja, Hannah Mainland, Hannah McCoy, Hannah Noble, Hannah Taplin, Harriet 'cidergirl' Stewart, Harriet McDougall, Harriet Rose Foulcer, Harriet Wood, Harry Barrow, Harry Holmes, Harry Price, Hattie Buttriss, Hattie Griffin, Hattie Taylor, Haydn Whiteside, Hayhay Giles, Hayley 'Laylee' Moore, Hayley Ash, Hayley Baker-Lartey, Hayley Butler, Hayley Gillett, Hayley McAllister, Hayley Parish, Hayley Tutte, Hazel Smith, Hazel Snelling, Heather B, Heather Leach, Helen Lawrence, Helen O'boyle, Helle Abelvik-Lawson, Henry A K Smith, Henry Clayton, Henry Dingle, Henry Flitton, Henry Humphreys, Herbi-Dacious, Hermione Duncan, Herve All, Hiro Inoue, Hocus Pocus, Hollie Burnett, Holly 'Penny' Farthing, Holly Berry, Holly Ellen Tedford, Holly Higham, Holly Nolan, Holly Saunders, Hugh Cosmo Paulley, Hugo Maia, Iain Wright, Ian Bonner, Ian Foss, Ian Jones, Ian Short, Idiojet, Iggy Davis, Imogen Lewis, Imogen Lily Page, Irul Yanto, Iskra Rebel-Katz, Isobel Lamb, IW Chronicle, Izzie Fowler, Izzy Cosgrove, Izzy Davies, Jac Husted, Jacinta Busher, Jack Boggia, Jack Cregan, Jack Gaskell, Jack Kinsey, Jack Longmuir, Jack Yates, Jackie 8506, Jackie Henderson, Jackie Jones, Jacob Glenn, Jacob Rising, Jacques Morris, Jacqui Brown, Jade 'Rabbit-head' Gildersleve, Jade Goodbourn, Jaime Quayle, Jake Fleetwood, Jake Gaskell, Jake Morris, Jake Mullins, Jake Tyrrell, James Bell, James Brown, James Carter-White, James Chambers, James Chapman, James Dowdeswell, James Galbraith, James Hb Marks, James Micklethwait, James Murray, James Nafi Aslan Kenny, James Pollack, James Taylor, James Wells, Jamesy Chapman, Jamie 'Jules' Beaumont, Jamie Blount, Jamie Boynton, Jamie McPp Prendergast, Jamie Nother, Jamie Parker, Jamie Prattle, Jamie Sumpter, Jamie Thompson, Jane Miles, Janet Mary Clark, Janie Barker, Janine Parr, Janine Pixies Funk Phillipson, Jasmine McNiven, Jasmine Sultanah, Jason Carr, Jason Caulfield, Jason Dade, Jason Phillips, Jay Coates, Jay George, Jaylee Michelle Miguel, Jaymee Bundell, Jayne Cresswell, Jeff Corney, Jeff Herbertson, Jemma 'Derp' McGhee, Jen Newman, Jeni Smillie, Jennifer Jane Atkins, Jenny Meagher, Jess Breeze, Jess Clarke, Jess Goble, Jess Kempner, Jessi 'Gin Fox' Dimmock, Jessica Breeze, Jessica Carminha Castellino, Jessica Griffin, Jessica Hao, Jessica Hothersall, Jessica Kate Armstrong, Jessica Millar, Jessica Zoe Roth Lehmann, Jez Flynn, Jim Hanner, Jim Hutchins, Jimmy Tib Davies, Jo Fleetwood, Jo Gibbs, Jo Lee, Jo Pullen, Jo Redfearn, Joanna 'Joey' Morrison, Joanna Brothers, Joanna Courage, Joanna Eynon, Joanna Louise Griffin, Joanna Styran, Joanna Willard, Joanne Macpherson, Joao Baptista, Jodie Hill, Joe Boyne, Joe Corney, Joe Crockett, Joe Dawson, Joe Entwisle, Joe Ferreira, Joe Foster, Joe George Claridge, Joe Kelly, Joe McElroy, Joe Miles, Joe Roszkowski, Joe Songhurst, Joe Sudds, Joe Wallace, Joey Howe, John Christie, John E M Mortimer, John Heery, John Hindley, John Holman, John Maclean, John Morgan, John Pedro Domingas Robson, John Usher, Johnny Suetens, Jojo Lowes, Jon 'Paz' Parrish, Jon Draper, Jon Graur, Jon Sutton, Jon'Handy, Jonathan Adcock, Jonathan Billington, Jonathan Hadlow, Jonathan Jacob, Jonathan Morgan, Jonathan Tutt, Jonathan Winchurch, Jono 'wrongo' Sanford, Jordan Holland, Jordan Royl, Jorden Pennington, Joseph Edward Llyod-Pike, Joseph Luk, Josh Bratt, Josh Brown, Josh Fay, Josh Gillard, Josh Longley, Josh Murray, Josh Peverley, Josh Twigg, Joshua 'Jay' Hobbs, Joshua Hamlyn, Joshua Jay Lewis, Josie 'Pinchy' Wilson, Josy Tenger, Jox McRox, Judith Lyall, Julia Bourne, Julian Drew, Julie Roo Marlow, June Redding, K Sam Clack, Kara Peacegood, Karen Amanda O'Rourke, Karen Hughes, Karen Sims, Kasper Bowyer-Knight, Kate Emery, Kate Goddard, Kate K463, Kate Manning, Kate Osler, Kate Rose, Kate Taylor, Kathryn Hornsby, Kathryn Stewart, Katie Briggs, Katie Churchward, Katie Greswell, Katie Herring, Katie Mackinnon, Katie Martin, Katie Smith Lawlor, Katy 'Chink' Martin, Katy Greeno, Katy Waring, Kayli Campbell, Kaytee Matthews, Kea-ra 'Kev' Jackson, Keeley Jones, Keith Fremantle, Kelly Atkin, Kelly Blades, Kelly Jones, Kelly Mccreanor, Kelly Murphy, Kelly Pike, Kelly Woolnough, Kelvin Leigh, Kemi Aofolaju, Kerry Anne Elizabeth, Kerry Cunningham, Kerry Le Lievre, Kerry Lelliott, Kerry Van Stratton, Kev Gadd, Kev Grigor, Kevin Coats, Kevin Freddie Hamilton, Kevin McGarr, Kieran Sockett, Kim Hume, Kim Lorraine Jones, Kim Von Coels, Kimberley Sutherland, Kirstie McAllister, Kirsty Boringface Slack, Kirsty Leanne Rowan, Kirsty Malone, Kirsty Rowley, Kirsty West, Kirsty-Marie Hunt, Kris Aarre, Kris Reid, Kristan Trit Taylor, Kyle Ross, Laila Azid, Lairy Love, Laura 'Lemon' Simmons, Laura Butcher, Laura Dann, Laura Fittall, Laura Hemsley, Laura Henderson, Laura Marie Carr, Laura Palmer, Laura Parsons, Laura Payne, Laura Peart, Laura Sheppard, Laura Souter, Laura Wilkinson, Laura Wilmot, Laura-Lee Mulligan, Lauren Amor, Lauren Brown, Lauren Emily Dawkins, Lauren Hurlow, Lauren Lolly Medlock, Lauren Mills, Lauren Semplis, Laurie French, Lawrence Spr, Leànnà Scott, Leanne Morgan, Leanne Park, Lee Davies, Lee De Louche, Lee Habberley, Lee Hall, Lee Mushing, Lee Nesbitt, Lee Skag Trendy Taylor, Lee Vine, Leigh Travers, Leigh Wetherall, Lesley Blackburn, Lesley J Wilkinson, Levi Evans, Lewis Alexander Crowe, Lewis Raine, Lewis Renehan, Lexie Bell, Liam 'Gilly' Guilfoyle, Liam Big-Dave Patrick Craughwell, Liam Burbeary, Liam Dey, Liam Fray O'Connell, Liam Mark Green, Liam McKenna, Liam Robins, Liam Siddons, Lindon Phillips, Linsey Marshall, Linton Van-Barnes Esq., Linzi Mccaroll, Lisa, Lisa Cable, Lisa Jardine, Lisa Jenkins, Lisa King, Lisa Le Peurian, Lisa Luce, Lisa Thomson, Liss Beardmore, Little Kate, Liz Disney, Liz Rosethorne, Liza Paulley, Lizzie Barry, Lizzie Bielicki, Lizzie Hudson, Lizzy Irvine, Lois Jb, Louis Stacey, Louise Guinhut, Louise Hadden, Louise Moore, Louise Pearce, Louise Whiteley, Loulou Carter, Loz Eagle Russell, Luana Buratta, Lubo Arvai, Luci Foy, Lucia Dove, Lucy Clark, Lucy Clarkson, Lucy Davies, Lucy Grace Vaughan, Lucy Isaacs, Lucy Kane, Lucy Macartney, Lucy McGowan, Lucy Parrott, Lucy Poole, Lucy Sanderson, Luka Taraskevics, Luke Andrews, Luke Coleman, Luke Hutson, Luke Macartney, Luke Osborne, Luke Palmer Divers, Luke Watkeys, Lydia Edwards, Lydia Wooldridge, Lyn Bekker, Lynda Murray, Lynsay McCall, Lynsey Kay, Mad as a box of FROGS, Madara Ermansone, Maddi Almightyy, Madison Bird, Maisie Booth, Maisie Cousins, Malcolm Niekirk, Malcolm Stoney, Mandy Winter, Marc Job, Marc Leishman, Marco Isolato, Marcus Seller, Marie Dunbar, Marika Vaphiadis, Mark Berner, Mark Charlton, Mark Cook, Mark Dunn, Mark Edmonds, Mark Fell, Mark Le Feuvre, Mark Martin, Mark Phillips, Mark Rawson, Mark Robinson, Mark Tripp, Martin Beall, Martin Peart, Martin Perry, Martyn Owen, Mary Chang, Mary Marshall, Maryam Elhabti, Mat Evans, Matt Barrett, Matt Bonner, Matt Cartlidge, Matt Chambers, Matt Corlett, Matt Edwards,

Matt Gotel, Matt Hennem, Matt Lewis, Matt Lovatt, Matt McKittrick, Matt Pattison, Matt Sherlock, Matthew Bain, Matthew Coles, Matthew Gibbons, Matthew Gilbert, Matthew Henley, Matthew Hill, Matthew J Flynn, Matthew Robbins, Matthew Scott Perry, Matthew Sibson, Matthew Smith, Matthew Thompson, Matty Brown, Matty Burrow, Max Lightman Coltart, May Worvill, Megan Beech, Megan Flockhart, Megan Gawthorpe-Luton, Megan Inett, Megan Thomas, Mel Clark, Mel Katharine, Melissa Gallagher, Mersh Johnson, Mia Bayle, Michael Drewery, Michael George, Michael Hanvey, Michael Kitchen, Michael Mccourt, Michael Rees, Michael Renou, Michael Sullivan, Michele Louise Merchant, Michelle Aiken, Michelle Harding, Michelle Phelps, Michelle Tish Tilley, Mick Yates, Mike Chatziapostolou, Mike Ingram, Mike Ramsey, Mike Ruane, Mike Schofield, Mike Simmers, Mikey Poole, Miles Mlambo, Mimi-Amy Sweet, ⟨Miss Red⟩ [◉◉], Missy-Rose Marsh, MisterJingo, Molly Beanland, Molly Carroll, Molly Drury, Moni Capreece, Monster Trump, Myke Haycock, Nadia Laice, Naomi Butson, Nasq Marinova, Natalie Ann Earl, Natalie Harlow, Natalie McGuinness, Natalie Pullen, Natalie Rippingale, Natalie Smith, Natalie Victoria Cherry Bomb, Natasha Frances Gilbody, Natasha Poole, Natasha Vickers, Nathan Cook, Nathan Leigh Horrocks, Nathan True, Nathan Watt, Nathaniel Brown, Naza Yousefi, Neal Searle, Nefney Graham, Neil Hartley, Neil Moore, Neil Paczkowski, Neil Patchdidit Paczkowski, Neil Pickles, Ness Page, Ness Whyte, Ng Hui Hsien, Nia Delaney, Niall Connolly, Nic B-C, Nic Brain, Nic Pegg, Nick Cowan, Nick Gardiner, Nick Samson, Nick Styran, Nicola Clark, Nicola Edwards, Nicola Hamer, Nicola Llewellyn, Nicole Donnelly, Nikki Dowie, Nikki Hooper, Nikki Warrington, Nina Burgess, Nina Szulc, Ninetta Papaioanni, Noura Sultani, Nykesha Slater, Oli Johnson, Oli Saul, Oliver Edward Martin, Oliver Mihm, Oliver Pinnington, Oliver Watson, Olivia Bloom Davis, Olivia Hemingway, Olivia Robertshaw, Ollie Flint, Olly Salanson, Olwyn D, Omirin Peter Horlarmiedey, Oscar, Oscar Bone, Oski Cazique, Ottilie Rounce, Owen Longuet, Pacey James, Paddy Leese, Paddy Melia, Pamela Hague, Pamela Mclauchlan, Pandora Hall, Paris Louise Brown, Pat Mutraporn, Pat Tyrrell, Patricia Tillotson, Patrick McGahon, Patrick McMeekin, Patrick Moyses, Patsie Ruddell, Paul Barron, Paul Case, Paul Darnell, Paul Forrest, Paul Garvey, Paul Jenkin, Paul Kenny, Paul Lomas, Paul Pj Jawando, Paul Stevens, Paul Tort Howard, Paul Vibert, Paulinho Crabb, Penny Saunders, Perry Taylor, Pete Sparkle Sparkle Mercer, Peter Alexander Raine, Peter Croft, Peter Dickinson, Peter Eagers-Bee, Petra Lindenbaum, Pewag Morris, Phil Brown, Phil Cairns, Phil Flewty Lewty, Phil Le Brun, Phil Maxwell, Phil Taylor, Phil Van Donovan, Philip Bruce, Philip Jones, Philip Waller, Phoebe Cripps, Pip Mutraporn, Pirie Benjamin, Polly Hadley, Polly Warren, Poppy Price, Puke Latton, Rachael Carter, Rachael Moore, Rachael Moran, Rachael Walton, Rachel Cunliffe, Rachel Foster, Rachel Lee, Rachel Lucy Pearce, Rachel Maxwell, Rachel Moran, Raddi Parekh, Rae Mccamphill, Raquel Garcia Escudero Cifuentes, Rebecca Ashton, Rebecca Carey, Rebecca Green, Rebecca Langlois, Rebecca Saunders, Rebekah-Leanne McHale, Reuben Graham, Rhiannon Kings, Ria Mesny, Rich Airmiles, Richard Christian, Richard Lancaster, Richard Lee, Richard Marshall, Richard Topham, Richie Knight, Rick Le Dew, Riko London, Ripeka Templeton, Ro Greene, Rob Brighton, Rob Davis, Rob Nixon, Rob North, Rob Spencer, Rob Williams, Robbie Kelly, Robbie Stevens, Robbie Winstanley, Robbie Wood, Robert Jones, Robert Kane, Robert Mcdonagh, Robert Rawson, Roberta Goulao, Robin Smith, Robin Taylor, Robyn Johnson, Robyn Martin, Robyn Rooke, Roisin Bridget Scott, Ronnie James Davis, Rory Kenyon, Rory Maltwood Marshall, Ros Saunders, Rosemary Fallon, Rosie Deane, Rosie Hope Kerr, Rosie Stone, Ross Altringham, Ross Carey, Ross Thomson, Ross Wings Myers, Roy Houston, Ruaraidh Mackay, Rudie Damijo, Rupert Wood, Russell Smith, Ruth Cannavan, Ruth Gwillim, Ruth Towle, Ry Robson, Ryan Christopher, Ryan Evans, Ryan Everton, Ryan Martin, Ryan Pinglaux, Ryan Tate, Ryan Thomas, Ryan Tolley,

Sabrina Mariana, Sadie Jane Pattinson, Sakura Yami, Saliha Lile Gurda, Sally Bremner, Sally Golightly, Sally McVay, Sally Sherlock, Sam 'Timmy' Verissimo, Sam Barham, Sam Beckley, Sam Benson, Sam Buucs Arnold, Sam Catt, Sam Cleare, Sam Dillon, Sam Jackson, Sam Mcgurk, Sam O'Dwyer, Sam Peach, Sam Phillips, Sam Rawlings, Sam Tye, Sam Tyrrell, Sam Willetts, Samantha Ernie Pinder, Samantha Jane Donaldson, Samantha Jane Lewis, Samantha Lear, Samantha Shore, Sammy Boobinz Lumsden, Sammy Schofield, Samuel Whittle, Samuell Waller, Sandra Bunting, Santa Oseniece, Sara Duff, Sara Leann Blackwell, Sara Stephenson, Sarah Baker, Sarah Bird, Sarah Buckley, Sarah Cornwell, Sarah DeThunderr Myrphty, Sarah Green, Sarah Hague, Sarah Harper, Sarah Holton, Sarah Jennings, Sarah Jones, Sarah L Spratley, Sarah Lowri McMahon, Sarah Paradise, Sarah Pickthall, Sarah Rallison, Sarah Shearer, Sarah Thomson, Sarah Walklett, Sarah Webster, Sarah Woods, Sasha Allenby, Saskia Johnson, Scott Bartlett, Scott McMaster, Scott Pullin, Sean Bell, Sean De Paul Mitchell, Sean Kennedy, Seb 'Sea Bass' Harris, Selene Alford, Sergei Renaissance Dimlic, Shan Pan, Shanice Willoughby, Shannen 'Mckenzie' Lentle, Shannon O'Hare Leitch, Sharde Passoos, Sharon Mary Salmon, Shaun Fraser, Shaun Jaques, Shaun Wheatcroft, Sheila Hastings-Rose, Shelley Bullen, Sheryl Kinnison, Sian Davies, Sian George, Sian Mullard, Simon Barnfather, Simon Beverley-smith, Simon Fruin, Simon Kowalenko, Simon Piper, Skye Bensted, Smashers Phelp, Smelly Twat, Sophia Miller, Sophia Toson, Sophie Adamson, Sophie Celine Miller Ryall, Sophie Francisco, Sophie Gaffney, Sophie Gallagher, Sophie Goddard-Jones, Sophie Goodenough, Sophie Grohl Rice, Sophie Lourdes Knight, Sophie Nash, Sophie Preston, Sophie Rouse, Sophie Taylor, 'Soundsonic' Rhys Gaster, Sparkle Eye Pixelcake, Spencer Holmes, Spim Subfactory, Stacey 'Steak' Knights, Stacey Ainley, Stacey Rogers, Stacie Maindonald, Stella Jones, Stella Peart, Steph Kelsey, Steph Park, Stephanie Briggs, Stephanie Hodge, Stephanie Remers, Stephanie Robinson, Stephanie Sapphire Keeley, Stephanie Thorndycraft, Stephanie Warrilow, Stephanie Wood, Stephen Dennis Baxter, Stephen Honeyball, Stephen Innes, Stephen Irving, Stephen Lloyd, Steve Bear, Steve Biddle, Steve Dunbar, Steve Hatch, Steve Hood, Steve Lewington, Steven Duffy, Steven Kelly, Steven Wright, Stevie Carter, Stevie Doc, Stewart Bywater, Stewart Futureproof Brookman, Stewart Hunter, Stuart MuddyFunkstarr Butler, Stuart Proudfoot, Stuart Wilmot, Sus Davy, Susie Brown, Susie McWilliams, Suzie Patrick, Tamara Brown, Tamarah Green, Tamsin Roberts, Tansy Sheppard, Tanya Bootsy, Tarryn Jade Blackwood, Tatch Man, Tattooed Mummy, Tavis Russell, Teddy Eastoe, Tendai Taruvinga, Teresa O'Neill, Terry Groves, Terry Tibbs Louise, Tessa McGrath, Tex Healy, Tezz Haywood, Thea Adelaide May, Theo Thompson, Thirzie Morton-Parker, Thom Gough, Thomas Daniel Swan, Thomas Hemsley, Thomas McGowan, Thomas Wilson, Tiffany Landamore, Tilly Henderson, Tim Dutton, Tim Rich, Tim Wong, Tina Mcardle, Tina Rollo, Tobiarse Michael Fforrdd, Toby Dobson Walsham, Toby John, Tom 'Moose' Haslam, Tom Andrew Turtle, Tom Bryant, Tom Gaskell, Tom Harvey, Tom Hemmings, Tom Hendry, Tom Johnson, Tom Molyneux, Tom O'Dwyer, Tom Robson, Tom Smith, Tom Stevenson, Tom Stewart, Tom Wells, Tom Wills, Tome Kinnear, Tomos Jones, Toni Heron, Toni James, Tony Ferreira, Tora Rebecca Rose, Tracey Borg, Tracey Percy, Tracey-lee Scully, Tracie Ann Large, Tracy Bonnar, Tracy Percy, Trevor Byrne, Trevor Seery, Tunde Awolaja, Vaughan Condron, Verity Ball, Vicki Louise Grant, Vicky Beercock, Vicky Emu Allen, Vicky Machon, Vicky Walker, Victoria K Morgan, Victoria Valius, Viv Youell, Wade Le Marquand, Warren Michael Berchie, Warren Sayer, Wayne Smith, Wee Liz, Fun, Laughter & Good Times…., Will Burdge, Will Dunn, Will-I Am'not Cosgrove, William Holden, William Mulvaney, Winston Swarley, Witty Cow, Wolfgang Alexander Sherlock, Xiao Zhu, Yeohan Kim, Zac Tyler, Zanne Lyttle, Zara Heath, Zena Taluhla Gardner, Zoe Edwards, Zoe Edwards, Zoe Fergus-Smith, Zoe Hooper, Zoe Middleton…

@_MissMiranda, @Akiki1028, @al_green, @AlanHostage, @AlexAllTimeLow, @Amy_Minor, @andyfairclough, @andynuttall, @AngelAnders, @ASOS_Laurafleur, @Baby_Tapir, @babz54321, @badjacket, @BellaLewisSmith, @bemyfirecracker, @BethhN, @blogmywiki, @blueskies, @BMWavesBlog, @bowdie, @BPJ_21, @calvinharris, @CapnDee, @carolineflack1, @Chard0301, @CharlotteSays, @cmcquillan, @CreativeFred, @D20E, @danwootton, @deb_max, @deemodha, @deslotted, @disastrid, @dizzycoolmellow, @DJDub, @doorlydj, @druidess, @duncmck7, @EllaLouisaS, @elzz_x, @erolalkan, @fifimurphy, @foxyhlc, @fuckity_fuck, @gashdigital, @gdpreston, @gibbinss, @GlastoWatch, @Grazia_Live, @gregallon, @gregfoot, @GuyLodge, @hattythomas, @Heathrow06, @henweb, @hltordoffUK, @hollieparade, @honosutomo, @Hulluna, @iamrachelharris, @IanClem, @iknowdavehouse, @iskrastrings, @Jack_McMullen, @jameelajamil, @jaydeadams, @jessicadoyle77, @joebemo, @joemuggs, @jokerunning, @jollyboysmusic, @JonasHalo, @jonesin4words, @jonoread, @joshmeatsix, @kesterbrewin, @KindersK, @Kirstena24, @KrystalGee, @LakesAdam, @LauraDemetriou, @linkcontrast, @lisaannewright, @Liss_anne, @LostBoyzClubE, @lottieLVATT, @luckynumbermus, @maryannehobbs, @maryviolet, @mattpark, @Maxmeatsix, @mharwood62, @midgeure1, @mirandacanfly, @Miss_Cakehead, @MPisthename, @nathanGallagher, @newgroovers, @nickystanding, @nilerodgers, @nippy_sweetie, @NomDeGuerre, @Pamela1606, @paraliztimelow, @paulcarvill, @paulcooper45, @paulefoster, @Peezza, @PhotoSonny, @producerneil, @ProjectMidnight, @PunksJumpUp, @rachel_reyn, @raemi3, @rasta4eyesuk, @REGYATES, @ricey747, @robbieflash, @robdabank, @Roveer, @rudyska, @sagray16, @sallyanna, @samueldjackson,

@sarahlouise152, @sarahwale, @SaritaBorge, @Scotty_SB, @seedrecords, @skiddle_com, @smallmancomplex, @sodpenguin, @soul_of_twit, @steamrunner, @SteveChortle, @stevencooperdj, @T_Sex, @t_t_t_tom, @The_Ameera, @the_style_queen, @TiernanDouieb, @TinyNat, @tiraybould, @Toolyboy, @topmanctrl, @TotalGuitar, @txteva, @UnaMullally, @vf, @zzzzeph,

Festival Annual Photographers: Jane Anderson (currentstate.co.uk/), Steve Bliss (stevebliss.blogspot.com), Jonny Baker (flickr.com/photos/jonnybaker), Chris James Edwards (chrisjamesedwards.com), Victor Frankowski (victorfrankowski.com), Matt Golowczynski (flickr.com/photos/golawola), Angelique Gross (angeliquegross.com), Tamsin Isaacs (styledisco.com), Felix Kunze (felixkunze.com), Monika Magiera (monikamagiera.blogspot.com/), Berni Martin (flickr.com/photos/bernimartinjersey), Alfie Maun (flickr.com/photos/first_aid_kit), Oscar May (oscarmay.com), Karl McCaughey (karlmcc.com), Caroline Michael (fotofillia.com) Jessie Simmons (jessiesimmons.com), Marco Spreca (cargocollective.com/marcospreca), Erik Srpek (rikolicious.com), Dan Wilton (danwilton.co.uk), and the IU Team. Designed by Rob Jones (renjones.co.uk).

Conceived, created and published by Independents United: Polly Aspinall, Clare Beaumont, Rachel Bishop Sunter, Ruth Clarke, Katherine Craughwell, Andrea Ferraz, Shevaun Haviland, Josh Jones, Frank Lampen, Bobby Mutraporn, Shilen Patel, Rob Povey, Becks Robertson, Nick Roe, Katie Shearer, Jon Thompson, Melissa Waters. **Online Editors:** Bobby Mutraporn and Nick Roe. Edited by Josh Jones and Frank Lampen.

With thanks to:

Sophie Rouse, James Howard, Amy Bliss, Katie Morrison, Bexy Cameron and all at MySpace; Kimberly Shilton, Fee Gilfeather, Stuart Fowkes and all at Oxfam; Clive Dickens, Clare Baker, Cat Macdonald, Llia Apostolou and all at Absolute Radio; John & Caroline Giddings, Lindsay Weatherston, Julia Barratt and all at Solo; Melvin Benn, Tania Harrison, James Kent, Sally Gill, Holly Jones and all at Festival Republic; Bruce Hay, John Hughes, Ziggy Gilsenan and all at Get Involved; Rob and Josie da Bank and all at Sunday Best; Ben Turner; Katrina Larkin and all at The Big Chill; Andrew Soar, Lyndsey Gates and all at Idea Generation; Gill Nightingale, Lucy Andrews and all at Cream; Marcus Thistleton and all at Live Nation; Alex Darling, Matthew Collier and all at LD Communications; Vicky Beercock, Kate Osler, and all at Angel Music Group; Julian Butterfield, Clare Lusher and all at Lovebox; Jenny Fairweather, Kate Arrowsmith and all at Taylor Herring; Katie at Bang On PR; Keong Woo at Family Ltd; Jo Vidler and all at Secret Garden Party; Siobhan O'Dowd and all at POD; Deirdre Crookes at LH Publicity; Hugo Tracey and all at Beach Break Live; Louise Roberts; Warren Le Sueur and all at Jersey Live; all at Shambala; Loren Gould at Mission Media; Holly de Sylva and Anna

Wade at DeSylva PR; Alex Trenchard, Tom O'Meara and all at Standon Calling; Alison Hall and all at the Glastonbury Press Office; Geoff Ellis and all at DF Concerts / TITP; Claire Ruddock, Emma Costello, Paul Rice, Kirstie Macdonald and all at Material MC; Jim King and all at Loud Sound; Laura Barette and all at Cake; Maztec Ltd for V Festival Hylands Park; Roseclaim Ltd for V Festival Weston Park; Rosie Deane and all at AEG Live; Charlie Caplowe and Dani at Press Counsel; Tom Baker, Jack Thomas and all at Field Day / Eat Your Own Ears; Shakira Fullwood-Gayle and Paul Kennedy at The Zeitgeist Agency; Alex Lee Thomson and Karen Johnson at Orbit PR; Adam Sagir and all at The Noise Cartel; Tom Jenkins at Cypher PR; Jeff Gray at Lock N Load Events; Katy Wickremesinghe and all at Freud Communications; Wayne Hemingway; Neil Barnes; Natalie Bennett; Katie Gerber; Jonathan Jacob; Nick Farnhill at Poke; Valdemar Domingos at Dentsu; Charlie Druce at Coasthouse; Steve Hatch and Ann Wixley at Mediaedge: CIA; Katie Rochester at Hill and Knowlton; Lindsay Nuttall; Rob Wilson and all at Lost & Found; Matt the Hat, Tristram Shackerley-Bennett and all at the Inflatable Church; Jason, Justin, Tori, Steve, Kieran and all at CC-Lab.

isleofwightfestival.com
Seaclose Park
10th – 13th June 2010
Capacity: 55,000

Isle of Wight

@gashdigital Arrived at IOW Festival in glorious sunshine! Finally chilling out after a manic week. Lush! Roll on the footie

11

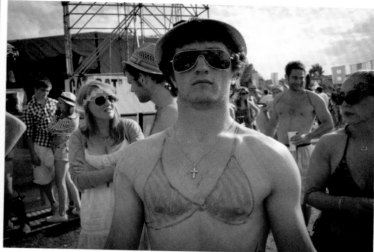

@MPisthename Hit the first night hard!! Is it too early for a cider? #IOW

@nickystanding **Music, cider, brilliant sunshine must be IOW festival, fun fun fun :-)**

@ASOS_Laurafleur There is an effing cheese counter backstage at #IOW. Oh, and florence welch is kicking about, talking to radio 1 but whatevs, there's CHEESE

@danwootton There is a mass exodus from the main stage to the football! #IOW

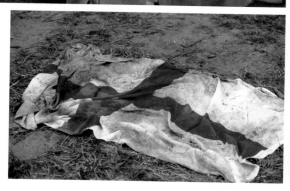

@midgeure1 **IOW festival a huge success all round. 60000 people having a party and embracing music and not just the perceived 'cool' stuff. Great.**

@sallyanna **My oesophagus is well and truely burnt. Ouch. #iow**

download festival.co.uk
Donigton Park, Leicestershire
9th – 13th June 2010
Capacity: 111,000

Download

@hltordoffUK i'm at
download festival and have
drank a bit too much.

@Chard0301 @DJChristianOC
And my son doesn't know about
his deceased snake, as he's
been at Download festival
since wednesday!

@Hulluna How much do i love download fest fans? awesome atmosphere, gonna see HIM soon.

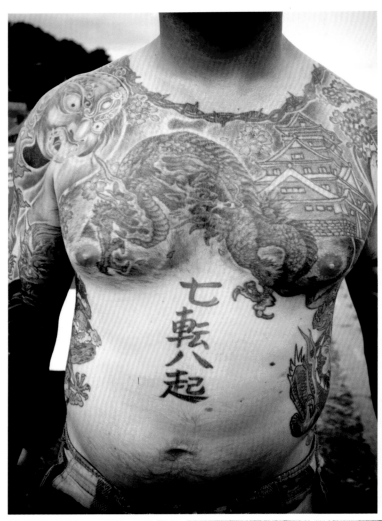

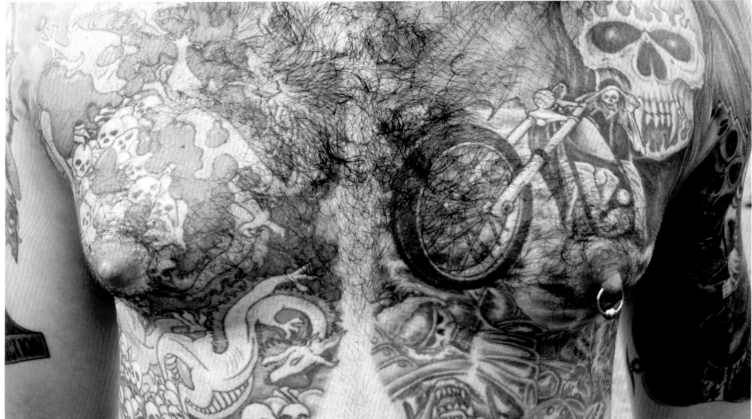

@Scotty_SB just got my first ever tattoo, bleeding a bit but it looks saweeeeeet :) heading off to @downloadfestival in a couple of hours, excited!

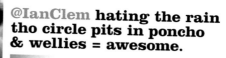

@IanClem hating the rain tho circle pits in poncho & wellies = awesome.

@TotalGuitar Q. What does Steven Tyler say at Download festival? A. Dude looks like it's raining! #DL2010.

@_MissMiranda is home from Download!! Sore, knackered, and frazzled but very proud of three amazing shows with Lucha Britannia...

rockness.co.uk
Clune Farm, Dores
11th – 13th June 2010
Capacity: 30,000

RockNess

@TiernanDouieb At Inverness and about to head to Rock Ness so cheerio Twitter till Sunday when I'll post pics of me holding Nessie's head and a glow stick.

@EdCassieMiller Bargain of the day... a camping mat for Rockness from the Pound Shop - a pound well spent!

@duncmck7 @zanelowe dude.
U ready to tear #rockness a
new one???

@LakesAdam Just had a
wet-wipe bath and feel good
as new! #rockness #fb

@skiddle_com Everyone's going a bit mental at #rockness, sun goes down and its mental! #skiddlerock

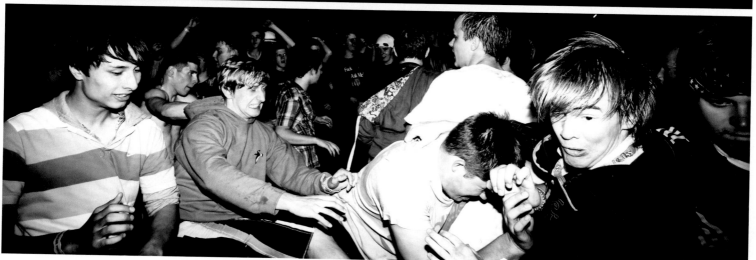

Glastonbury

SOFT ICE

5.0M
15FT

glastonburyfestivals.co.uk
Worthy Farm, Somerset
23rd – 28th June 2010
Capacity: 177,500

@disastrid "hm, a man in a dress talking to a carrot." #glasto

@GlastoWatch Hippie (Could
be Banksy or one of his mates!)
tries to tempt Prince Charles
into a drug deal at Glasto…

@paulcarvill I saw Gemma at Glastonbury watching a bloke walk around on stilts for about THREE HOURS. She couldn't believe how MAD he was!

@JonasHalo Help me. I'm on acid up some stilts in the lavender field. This is an emergency. Stop the Twitter and help. #glasto

@sodpenguin This year's Glastonbury fancy dress theme is slightly sunburned middle class berk in a straw hat.

@sagray16 Too hot at #glasto.
Found shade nears mens urinals.
I have no shame it's too hot.

@jokerunning Can you get sunburn through a layer of baked on sweat and dust? #glastonbury

THE ONLY MUD IN GLASTONBURY

LOOKOUT DAMP PATCH

@AngelAnders Theres no mud at Glastonbury. The sunburn lines are spectacular and the kids love the show! X

@joebemo I'll be back at Glasto next year. Football is nothing, NOTHING, compared to Glastonbury.

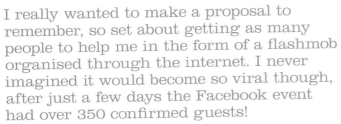

I really wanted to make a proposal to remember, so set about getting as many people to help me in the form of a flashmob organised through the internet. I never imagined it would become so viral though, after just a few days the Facebook event had over 350 confirmed guests!

I was a nervous wreck the whole day but it was worth every minute spent organising it. Thankfully the answer was yes or I may not have shown my face in public again! Thanks again to anyone reading this who helped out!

Mark Robinson

I have no idea how Mark managed to keep this a secret! It wasn't until the crowd shouted "Sarah will you marry me?" that I knew anything about it. At this point I think I burst into tears whilst also nodding my head!

Thankfully we were whisked up to the top of The Park tower, which was something I had wanted to do since we arrived. This year's festival is certainly one we will never forget!

Sarah Robinson née Hague

@andynuttall At risk of sounding ungrateful, could we please have some cloud and a breeze at #glasto

@deslotted it doesn't need a whole tweet, one word covers all aspects of #glasto. Hot. :)

@foxyhlc Made friends and am off to party in the stone circle #glasto ps i've pulled! Lol!

@deb_max **Even the dust has dust... #Glastonbury**

@druidess *Sits back against the altar feeling the magic of the stone circle wash over her, this was the place of her vision*

@AlanHostage Ahhhh glasto arcadia crew! That was frightening, exhilarating and amazing! Thanks so much. Could kiss the ground!

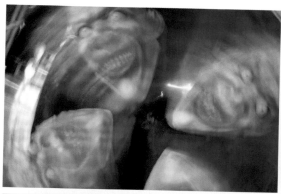

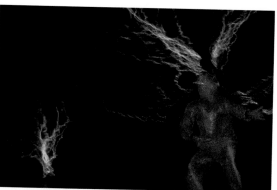

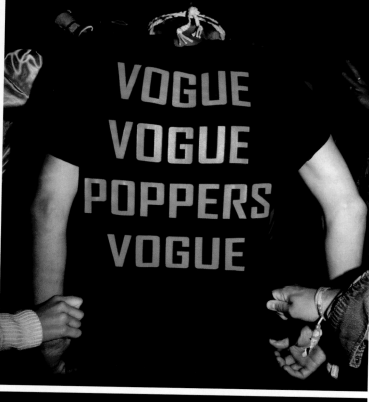

@PhotoSonny The flashing cube henge is one of the greatest festival instalations I've ever seen. #Glastonbury

@steamrunner #Glastonbury: An escape to the most incredible fantasy world made real. Amazing music. Fantastic friends. Great times. FTW!

@al_green **A Hot, dirty, smelly, crowded monster of a party with added eccentricity, elegance & absolutely amazing energy!**

@fuckity_fuck Sleep, tent, sun, walk, sit, cider, music, dawn repeat #glasto

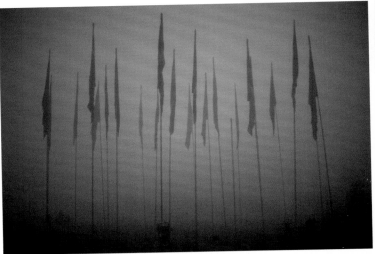

@robbieflash Last night was an absolute mad one. Shangri-La then Stone Circle til' dawn. #Glasto site was like a wasteland in the fog

@joemuggs I lost my mind at Glastonbury, felt better without it, left it there. Some poor sod will dig it up one day.

tinthepark.com
Balado, Kinross-shire
9th – 12th July 2010
Capacity: 85,000

T in the Park

@babz54321 Thought it was supposed to be raining at T in the Park but everyone's wearing sunglasses!

@TinyNat - **T in the Park = the most lovely, friendly and polite festival goers! Plus they know how to have a great time! =D**

**@CapnDee is having
T in The Park. Hell Yeah**

@D20E Is enjoying t in the park. Taking a break just now between acts. Thankfully the heavy rain stopped when music started!

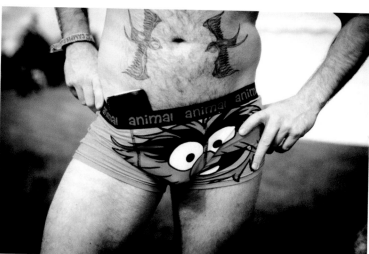

@maryviolet The crowd at T in the park seems to be an, erm, interesting mix...

@TheAmeera Enjoying all the love Scotland is getting right now cos of T in the Park Scottish people are awesome :D

@Kirstena24 There's really only one word do describe T in The Park... insane! D:

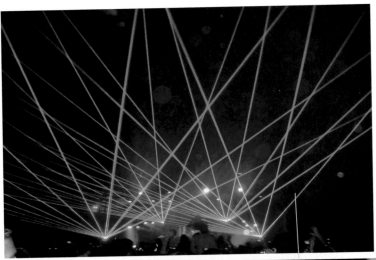

@Jack_McMullen **It's in a tent with random Scottish people. I like making new friends :) T in the Park!!! :D x**

@Peezza
**T in the park =
AWESOME!! :D**

**@Pamela1606 2nite is going
down as 1 of the best nites of
my life!! Loved every second of it.
Thank u T in the Park!!**

oxegen.ie
Punchestown Racecourse, Co Kildare
9th – 11th July 2010
Capacity: 80,000

Oxegen

@raemi3 **managed to burn my knees at oxegen this morning O.o**

@calvinharris Oxegen last night was the gig of my life...! I'm going back to London now. Not had very much sleep at all. All sorts of weirdness went on!?

Lounge on the Farm

loungeonthefarm.co.uk
Merton Farm, Canterbury
9th – 11th July 2010
Capacity: 7,000

@DJDub The kids may have meow meow but I prefer a nice cup of chai tea & a Portuguese custard tart, @DJYodaUK makin Lounge on the Farm BOUNCE!

@BMWavesBlog Lounge on the farm is the only festival where the main stage is in a huge cow shed and inflatable cows hang from the roof. Surreal.

latitudefestival.co.uk
Henham Park, Suffolk
9th – 11th July 2010
Capacity: 35,000

Latitude

To Tom Jones,
you are really
Sexy + i dedicate
this to you
Sarah x

@badjacket **Come on,
then, latitude toilets.
Let's see what you've got**

@smallmancomplex I just lied to someone and told them I was performing at Latitude so they helped me get to the front

@jonoread Phil Jupitus: "I have the Observer food monthly. A challenging wank for some but not for me" #latitude

create love and take heart beautiful world

Following the success of 2009's festival season, which saw 30,000 people at festivals paint themselves blue to join Oxfam's climate change campaign, 2010 had to be bigger and better. This year saw festival-goers at ten different festivals across the summer get henna tattoos stencilled on their knuckles, legs, backs, arms and faces, spelling out 'FAIR DEAL', with thousands of them joining the global movement of people who want those in poverty to be treated fairly in the face of climate change.

Since 1993 Oxfam has signed up the support of more than half a million people for their campaigns at festivals, tackling everything from global trade to climate change in the process.

oxfam.org.uk/festivals

lovebox.net
Victoria Park, London
16th – 18th July 2010
Capacity: 30,000

@gdpreston **Hip hop karaoke, dancing security guards - amazing! #lovebox**

@jessicadoyle77 At lovebox.
Never have I seen so many
animal-print jumpsuits.

@deemodha Lost my voice, last heard at Lovebox. If found please return.

@GuyLodge High point
of Lovebox yesterday:
Roxy Music, duh. Low point:
getting propositioned at
the urinals with a rather
too-intimate observation.

@nippy_sweetie Love in the
box, box lovin', Love the box,
#Lovebox eeeeek ♥

@NomDeGuerre At secret garden party! 75% naked 99% loved up

@samueldjackson In a cab with 5 strangers. I feel trashed. My feet are bleeding. What's secret garden party like? I'm going in the lake.

@bemyfirecracker Secret Garden
Party is like Disney for adults
with music. And less kids.

@kesterbrewin At Secret Garden Party. Various asylums been emptied here for the weekend.

@iskrastrings Arrived at The Secret Garden Party with @JonBilbrough. Everyone one is still asleep.

@newgroovers At secret garden party with me two strawberry shortbreads what a festival. Loving it I'm going to be the Strawberry king!!! Fact not fiction.

@KindersK Having the time of my life with george the tortoise, a large penguin and some awesome swing at secret garden party. #fb

@jameelajamil Secret garden party festival is amazing. Dancing all night like the daft baffoon I am... Heavenly.

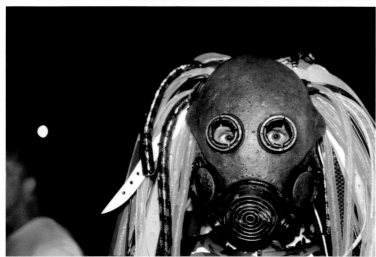

@luckynumbermus Secret garden party on a Sunday is like the last days if Rome - hmmm not sure about this one

@Roveer Funeral done.
On to Global Gathering
now! #GG10

@**CharlotteSays** I am dressed as a tiger dancing around a tent at Global Gathering

campbestival.net
Lulworth Castle, Dorset
30th July – 1st August 2010
Capacity: 28,000

@gregallon @billybragg very excited you will be telling my kids bedtime stories at camp bestival. Will feel like my life has come full circle.

@fifimurphy Outside lulworth castle watching marc almond at camp bestival

159

@blogmywiki Survived day 1 of Camp Bestival. After getting there on my own with 3 kids & getting tent up a can of cold beer has never tasted so sweet.

@nathanGallagher
Camp Bestival; the only festival where The Friendly Fires and Madness can be overshadowed by a middle-aged man in make-up called Mr. Tumble

@BellaLewisSmith wish the @campbestival app sorted my fancy dress #lastminute fancy dress #fail

@mharwood62 I am simultaneously the oldest child and the youngest adult at a festival. I think i'll come to camp bestival again.

@producerneil Someone in the camping is now playing La Isla Bonita at high volume. 'Camp' Bestival indeed

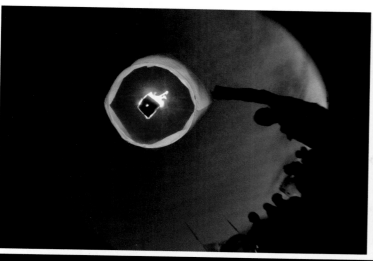

Sonisphere

uk.sonispherefestivals.com
Knebworth, Hertfordshire
30th July – 1st August 2010
Capacity: 55,000

@tlraybould Wheelchair crowd surfer at funeral for a friend on bohemia at #sonisphere

@KrystalGee
At sonisphere, disapointed by lack of mockable outfits

Field Day

fielddayfestivals.com
Victoria Park, London
31st July 2010
Capacity: 25,000

@vf Talking of sun, big props (does anyone say that anymore?) to the guy next to us who just drank sun tan lotion at #fieldday. Tasty

underagefestivals.com
Victoria Park, London
1st August 2010
Capacity: 10,000

Underage Festival

@mirandacanfly: Underage was
immense, good music, good hair,
good jeans and lol mosh pits :P

@ricey747 Fuck, these kids know how to bounce! @HadoukenUK #Underage

@elzz_x mm i might actually start using twitter now, went underage festival today and few singers gave out their usernames, addaddadd<3

bigchill.net
Eastnor Castle, Herefordshire
5th – 8th August 2010
Capacity: 40,000

The Big Chill

@soul_of_twit Apologies for any offence caused by me eating my noodles crosslegged at the main stage whilst still in my Spencer Tunick 'costume' #bigchill

@Miss_Cakehead Perfect
weather for 1000's of naked
people to be body painted
& lie in a field at Big Chill
for Spencer Tunick

@jollyboysmusic **Our Big Chill Festival performance was great. We had fun playing in front of an awesome crowd and a beautiful rainbow**

@linkcontrast Today I mostly ate falafel and listened to wobble #bigchill

@bowdie **Yay. Festivals! Where else can you get a marmite crumpet at one on a Sunday morning! #bigchill**

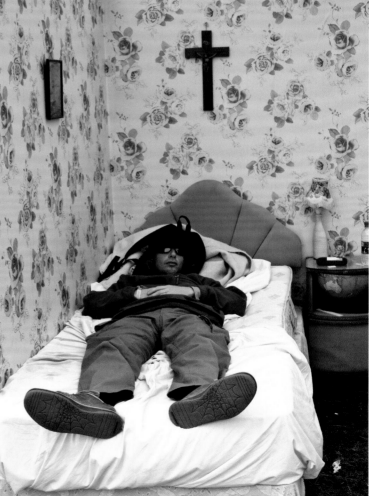

@mattpark Still at big chill, not dead, but close

standon-calling.com
Standon Lordship, Hertfordshire
6th – 8th August 2010
Capacity: 5,000

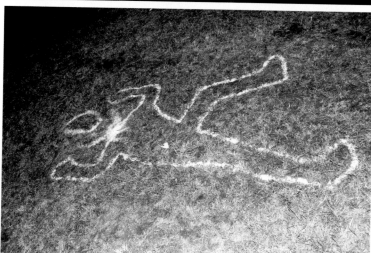

@lisaannewright All festivals should involve swimming and dog shows. Congrats Standon Calling. You win.

@henweb Standon Calling - you are on at 5pm. You will be doing a tap dance to the music of Mark Knopfler, followed by improv. Okay?

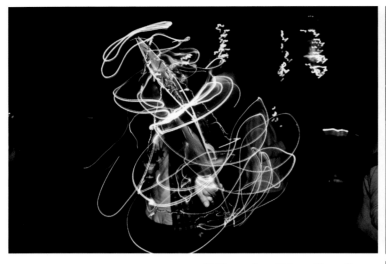

@Grazia_Live **Loving
Standon Calling festival
fashion: "funnies" - as in
funny sunnies - out in force**

Vintage at Goodwood

vintageatgoodwood.com
Goodwood Estate, Surrey
13th – 15th August 2010
Capacity: 17,500

@hattythomas
Amazing experience
vintage at goodwood!
My nannies rock!!

@sarahwale Enjoying Vintage
at Goodwood despite the rain.
Sandie Shaw et al & Faces good
last night. Currently drinking
tea, vintage people watching!

boomtownfair.co.uk
Stowe Landscape Gardens, Buckinghamshire
13th – 15th August 2010
Capacity: 5,000

Boomtown Fair

@T_Sex Topless trio debut
at Boomtown Fair was big.
No baby oil but still sexy.

@Baby_Tapir Wurzel time
@ Boomtown Fair

@iamrachelharris Went to my first festival this weekend - Boomtown Fair, and it was amazing! I'm in my festival finest here...

@rasta4eyesuk BOomTowN Fair 2010 = incredible

vfestival.com
Weston Park, Staffordshire
21st – 22nd August 2010
Capacity: 85,000

@txteva Cheesy bacony garlic bread and seasick steve... Awesome! #Vfest

@paulefoster Vfest update: two beers down, one burger and chips and have seen feeder!

@rachel_reyn #vfest red camping. bad idea getting drunk before erecting the tent. haha. erect.

@paulcooper45 I'm at #vfest and I need a poo, is there an app for that?

@the_style_queen: Some one pray for the rain to go away!!!no shelter whilst queueing for toilets!!all about the champs bar though #VFestival

V Chelmsford

vfestival.com
Hylands Park, Chelmsford
21st – 22nd August 2010
Capacity: 87,500

@BethhN **Just watched palomafaith at the v festival chelmsford, flipping amazing!**

@Toolyboy **Day 2 at V. Maltesers milkshake for breakfast and little Pixie dancing on the stage. No rain yet in Chelmsford thank the sweet Lord.**

@Amy_Minor At V Chelmsford there seem to be a thing where everyone would shout Alan everywhere I was so confused :s

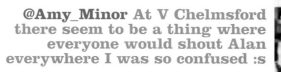

Akiko1028 あ、Hylands Park 結
構雨降ってるね… There's goes the
fear で最後ポコポコ観られるかな？
#vfestival

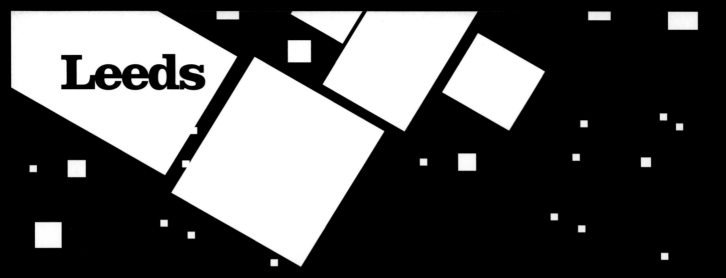

Leeds

leedsfestival.com
Bramham Park, Leeds
27 - 29 August 2010
Capacity: 69,999

@iknowdavehouse Hey Reading, it's sunny in Leeds!

@zzzzeph Take me down to Paradise City. Where the grass is green and the girls are pretty. @gunsandroses279 last night @leedsfest

@rudyska Woke up next to two random English girls and a friend, in an unknown tent this morning. Fair to say Leeds festival was fucking amazing.

@blueskies Incidentally, anyone who was at Leeds Festival tonight and didn't see The Libertines has comprehensively lost the game of life.

readingfestival.com
Little John's Farm, Reading
27 - 29 August 2010
Capacity: 86,999

Reading

@LauraDemetriou Reading is flipping amazing. Great weather and loads of mud and creepy guys asking if they can spoon me.

@REGYATES Nothing better than watching a hot overdressed girl drop in the mud. #readingfestival

@sarahlouise152 **Reading fest is my happy place, I wish it existed every day of the year. #readingfestival**

@gibbinss wow reading fest = too amazing for words O.o my legs are just one big bruise but everything was worth it like woah I can't even describe it

@EllaLouisaS Reading Fest.. amazinggg today! Dizzee Rascal, Crystal Castles, Pendulum, The Futureheads and The Libertineeeesssss were...amazing!!! :)

259

@joshmeatsix Reading festival, my mind has been blown! Thanks to everyone that gave me a high 5 by crowd surfing. Sorry if you got hurt. Love ya

@Maxmeatsix Reading festival today should be rad, awesome bands and awesome people!!!

@hollieparade At reading festival, covered in beer. With a possible broken rib, watching the drums having a fucking amazing time!

@SaritaBorge Overwhelmed to see main crowd at reading from side of stage. Paramore frikkin ROCKIN IT. What it's all about dudes. Immense.

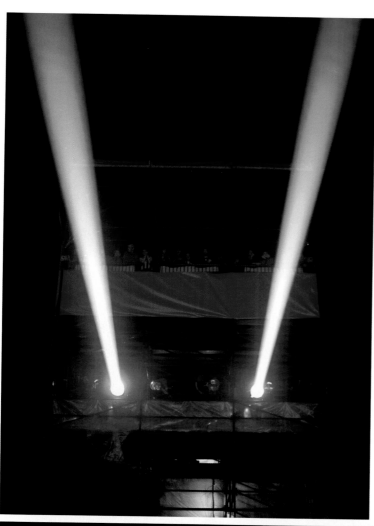

@honosutomo "Every night my dream's the same." Arcade Fire are so far and above anything else at #readingfestival that it's almost humbling.

@lottieLVATT Any tips on how to get anywhere near the front of the main stage at Reading? Haha.

@AlexAllTimeLow **The defining point of Reading fest is to go down on a stranger in a muddy tent. Live the dream!**

shambalafestival.org
Secret location, Northamptonshire
26th – 30th August 2010
Capacity: 7,000

Shambala

@seedrecords Antoni Maiovvi plays Shambala festival tonight. You'll dance so hard your legs will fly off and your head will explode.

@cmcquillan Trending at this year's Shambala: bear costumes and crutches as accessories. Hedonism, diversity, eccentricity and the bearded kitten!

L.E.D Festival

ledfestival.net
Victoria Park, London
27th & 28th August 2010
Capacity: 20,000

@erolalkan Creamfields
completely off the grid
thank u xxxxxxxxxx

@djmiken **Creamfields is sick.
Already seen 7 deadmau5 shirts
and a head lol**

RuthieStar So tired!
Creamfields took it out of me...
I'm getting too old for this!

@diodesign #creamfields green lasers and glowsticks make anyone a great dancer. Ask anyone here. PS Haven't heard out of the blue in 10yrs

South West Four

southwestfour.com
Clapham Common, London
28th – 29th August 2010
Capacity: 20,000

electricpicnic.ie
Stradbally Hall, Co. Laois
3rd – 5th September 2010
Capacity: 32,500

Electric Picnic

@UnaMullally Electric Picnic isn't so much a music festival than an outdoor arena where all of your exes decide to collide.

@stevencooperdj Uh factor 30 is not strong enough for my pale face neck all burnt! And I've been applying every frigging hour :/ @electricpicnic

Bestival

bestival.net
Robin Hill Country Park, Isle of Wight
9th – 12th September 2010
Capacity: 48,000

@maryannehobbs word from @robdabank himself.. deffo no need for wellies at Bestival today.. no mud on site.. :)

@gregfoot Campervan? Check. Fancy dress? Check. 7 mates up for a weekend of partying? Check. Time for Bestival!!

@carolineflack1 Bestival
highlights.... Flaming lips...
Mumford...smurf outfits...
comfy mattresses and nice
friendly people..happy x

@jaydeadams Last night was messy. @bestival today's weather has been amazing again.

@andyfairclough Feeling fragile after partying till 4am. Fancy dress Saturday at #bestival might be a struggle.

@nilerodgers **My Fairy Godmother at Bestival granted me 3 wishes-ALL came true!**

@topmanctrl The Correspondents:
Jovial dandy with a good line
in running man. Surprising
MC skills and a mini travelator

@LostBoyzClubE #bestival was one of the best weekends of my life, sunset with chic on the sunday evening was a moment..

@doorlydj Let my lack of tweets speak volumes about how much fun I had last night! Super big ups to @RobdaBank They dont call it BESTival for nothing!

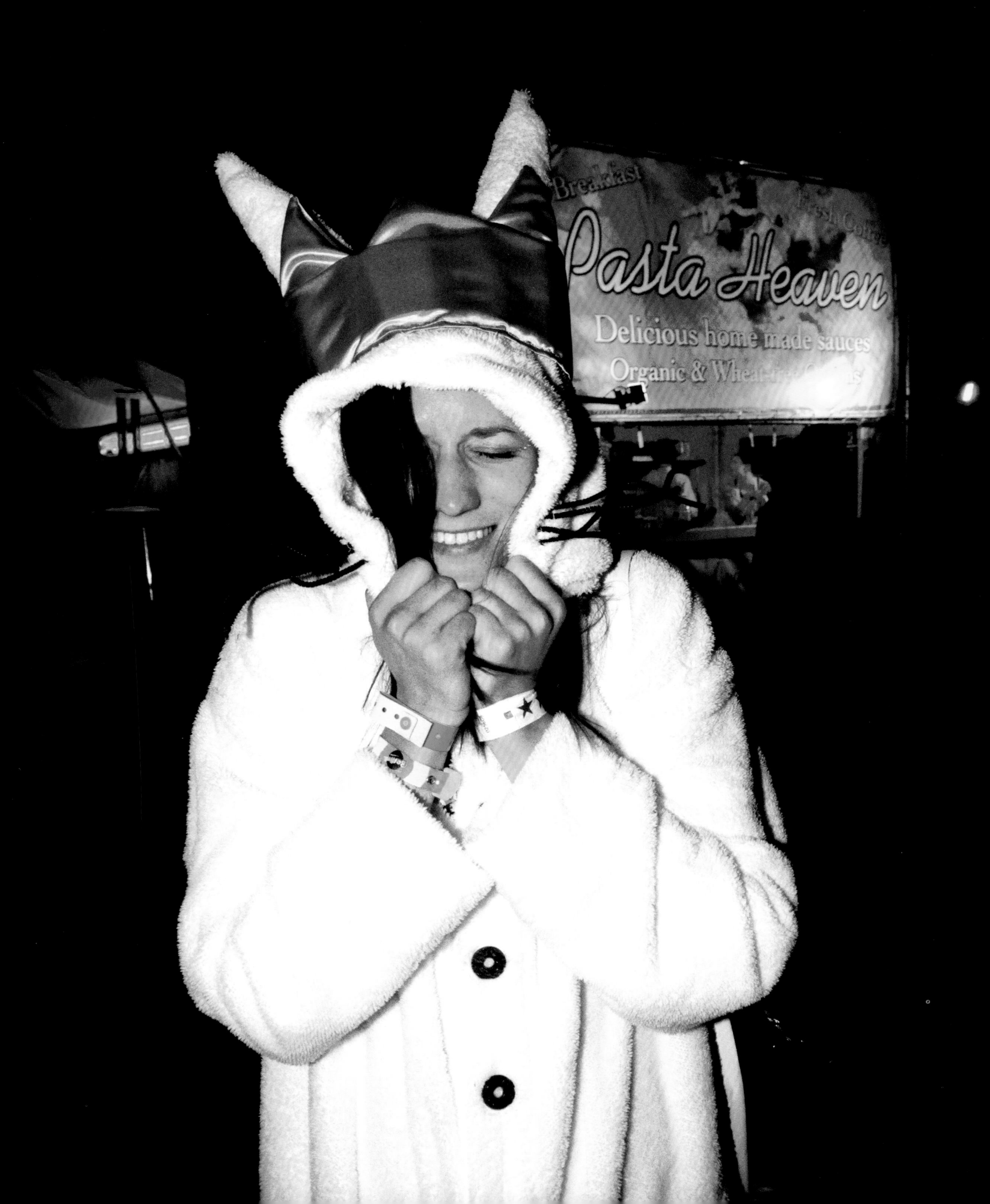
Breakfast
Pasta Heaven
Delicious home made sauces

@robdabank Massive thanks to all @Bestival crew who made it our best one yet... reeeesssssppeeeccckk! Can I change my pants now pls :)

Photo Credits:

Isle of Wight
p8-9: Frank Lampen for Festival Annual
p10 top: Oscar May (oscarmay.com); all others: FL
p11-12: Oscar May
p13: middle right: Oscar May; all others: FL
p14-18: all: FL
p19: bottom left: Monika Magiera (monikamagiera.blogspot.com/); all others: FL
p20: Oscar May
p21: FL

Download
Photographed for Festival Annual by Dan Wilton (danwilton.co.uk)
Additional photos:
p24: Pewag Morris
p26: left: Pewag Morris
p34-35 all photos: Tom Medwell (tommedwell.com)

RockNess
Photographed for Festival Annual by Steve Bliss (stevebliss.blogspot.com)
Additional photos:
p44: top right: Nic B-C
p47: middle right: Natalie Bennett; bottom right: Nic B-C
p50-53: Steve Bliss & Natalie Bennett

Glastonbury
p54-55: Nick Roe for Festival Annual
p56: top and bottom right: Dan Wilton for Festival Annual; bottom left: NR
p57: top left: NR; top right: DW; middle and bottom: Steve Bliss for Festival Annual
p58-59: Marc Sethi (flickr: sethmondo)
p60: DW
p61: right bottom: DW; all others NR
p62: top left: NR; top right: Nic B-C; middle: Marc Sethi ; bottom: DW
p63: top right SB; all others: DW

p64: top: NR, bottom left: Dave Beveridge; bottom right: SB
p65: top: NR; bottom: Marc Sethi
p66: DW
p67: left column top, right column middle and bottom: SB; left column bottom and right column top: NR
p68: top right: Andrea Innocenti; all others: NR
p69: DW
p70-71: all: NR
p72: SB
p73: top: Marc Sethi; middle and bottom: SB
p74: DW
p75: top left: DW; bottom left: Dave Beveridge; top and bottom right: Marc Sethi
p76: DW
p77: SB
p78: top: Marc Sethi; middle: NR; bottom left and right: DW
p79: top left: Dave Beveridge; top right: Sophie Goddard; middle left: Matthew Smith; middle right and bottom left: DW; bottom right: SB
p80: top and bottom left, middle right: Matthew Smith; top right: Kate Greswell; middle left: Dave Beveridge; bottom right: Nic B-C
p81: left column top: Nic B-C; left middle: Elly Wakeling; left bottom: Marc Sethi; right column top: Hannah Lanfear; second: Dave Beveridge and Richard John Mattingley; third and bottom: Dave Beveridge
p82: SB
p83: top: DW; bottom: SB
p84: top left, bottom left and top right: SB; all others: DW
p85: DW

T in the Park
p86-87: Oscar May for Festival Annual
p88: all: OM
p89-90: Steve Bliss for Festival Annual
p91: OM
p92: left: Michelle Tilley; right: OM
p93: OM

p94: top and bottom right: SB; bottom left: Michelle Tilley
p95: top left and bottom right: OM; top right: SB; bottom left: Michelle Tilley
p96: top left: Natalie Bennett; all others: SB
p97: Natalie Bennett
p98: top: Robyn Martin; middle and bottom: SB
p99: top & middle: SB; bottom: OM
p100-101: SB

Oxegen
Photographed for Festival Annual by Karl McCaughey (karlmcc.com)

Lounge On The Farm
p106: Victor Frankowski (victorfrankowski.com)
p107: all: Nick Roe for Festival Annual

Latitude
p108-109: Jessie Simmons (jessiesimmons.com) for Festival Annual
p110: top and middle left, middle and bottom right: Jane Anderson (currentstate.co.uk) for Festival Annual; bottom left and top right: JS;
p111: JS
p112: top: Steve Malpass (shutterfox.co.uk); bottom left: JS; bottom right: JA
p113-115: all: JA
p116: top left: Steve Malpass; all others: JA
p117: middle: JS; all others JA
p118-119: all: JA
p120-121: Steve Malpass
p122: all: JA
p123: Steve Malpass

Lovebox
p124-125: Tamsin Isaacs (styledisco.com) for Festival Annual
p126-127: all: Angelique Gross (angeliquegross.com) for Festival Annual
p128-131: Marco Spreca

(cargocollective.com/marcospreca) for Festival Annual
p132: top left and bottom right: MS; all others: AG
p133: top right: Bartek Szadura (bartekszadura.weebly.com); all others: AG
p134: MS
p135: top left and bottom right: MS; middle left and top right: TI; bottom left: AG

Secret Garden Party
p136-137: Tamsin Isaacs
p138-139: Frank Lampen for Festival Annual
p140: Dave Gibbons (davegibbons.org.uk)
p141: FL
p142: Tamsin Isaacs
p143: Jayde Adams
p144-145: all: FL
p146: Dave Gibbons
p147-149: all: FL
p150: middle left: Jayde Adams; all others: FL
p151: FL

Global Gathering
Photographed for Festival Annual by Monika Magiera
Additional photos:
p154: bottom right: Charlotte 'ElectroFudge' Fitzgibbon
p155: top left and right: Charlotte 'ElectroFudge' Fitzgibbon; middle right: Andrew Blair

Camp Bestival
p156-159: Angelique Gross for Festival Annual
p160: Marco Spreca for Festival Annual
p161: top and bottom right: MS; middle: AG; bottom left: Fran Jones (flickr: franjones | hughart.co.uk)
p162-163: AG
p164-165: Jayde Adams
p166: top left and right, bottom: AG; middle: MS
p166: top left and right, bottom: AG; middle: MS

p167: top left: Hannah Morgan (flickr: fionchadd); top right: AG; middle: Ian Pearce (flickr: AntSizedMan); bottom: MS
p168: all: Jayde Adams
p169: top left: Hannah Morgan; top right: Alicia Talikowska (aliciayolanda.wordpress.com); bottom: MS

Sonisphere
Photographed for Festival Annual by Oscar May
Additional photo:
p175: top left: Sarah Murphy

Field Day
Photographed for Festival Annual by Erik Srpek (rikolicious.com)

Underage Festival
Photographed for Festival Annual by Alfie Maun (flickr: first_aid_kit)

The Big Chill
p182-183: Jessie Simmons for Festival Annual
p184: top and bottom left, bottom right: Jonny Baker (flickr: jonnybaker); middle left and top right: JS
p185: top and middle left, top right: JS; bottom left, middle and bottom right: JB
p186: Victor Frankowski
p187: all: JB
p188: top and middle left: JS; bottom left, top and bottom right: JB
p189: JB
p190: top right: JS; all others JB
p191: all: JB
p192: Jamie Boynton (fictionalfuture.com)
p193: top and middle left: JS; bottom left and right: JB
p194-195: JB

Standon Calling
p196-197: Jim Hanner
p198: top and bottom right: Tamsin Isaacs for Festival Annual; bottom left: Jim Hanner
p199: bottom left: Jim Hanner; all others TI
p200: TI
p201: all photos: Jim Hanner
p202: middle: Jim Hanner; all others: TI
p203: Jim Hanner

Vintage at Goodwood
All photos: Nick Roe for Festival Annual

Boomtown Fair
All photos by Matthew Smith

V Weston
p212-216: Frank Lampen for Festival Annual
p217: top left and right, bottom right: FL; middle left and right, bottom left: Nick Roe for Festival Annual
p218: FL
p219: top left: FL; all others: NR
p220: bottom left: NR; all others: FL
p221-223: FL

V Chelmsford
Photographed for Festival Annual by Matt Golowczynski (flickr: golawola)

Leeds
p232-234: Caroline Michael for Festival Annual (fotofillia.com)
p235: top left and right: CM; middle right: Nick Roe for Festival Annual; bottom left and right: Jon Thompson for Festival Annual
p236-237: CM
p238: top left and bottom right: CM; bottom left and top right: NR

p239: bottom left: JT; all others: CM
p240-242: CM
p243: top and bottom left, bottom right: JT; top and middle right: CM
p244-245: JT
p246: top left: JT; middle: NR; top right, bottom left and right: CM
p247: CM

Reading
p248-249: Oscar May for Festival Annual
p250-251: All photos: Felix Kunze for Festival Annual (felixkunze.com)
p252-253: All photos: OM
p254: top left and right, middle: FK; bottom left and right: OM
p255: top left: FK; top right and bottom: OM
p256: top left and bottom right: FK; bottom left and top right: OM
p257-267: all photos: FK

Shambala
All photos by Matthew Smith

L.E.D Festival
Photographed for Festival Annual by Chris Edwards (chrisjamesedwards.com)

Creamfields
All photos: Nick Roe for Festival Annual

South West Four
Photographed for Festival Annual by Chris Edwards

Electric Picnic
Photographed for Festival Annual by Karl McCaughey

Bestival
p288-291: Frank Lampen for Festival Annual
p292-293: Fay Woodford (flickr: specialf)
p294: All: FL
p295: top and bottom: FL; middle Nick Roe for Festival Annual
p296-299: All: FL
p300: top and bottom left: FL; top right: Victor Frankowski; bottom right: Tamsin Isaacs for Festival Annual
p301-302: FL
p303: TI
p304: middle left: TI; all others: FL
p305-306: FL
p307: top left and middle: FL; top right: Victor Frankowski; bottom: TI
p308-309: FL

EAST
AFRICA
safari in style

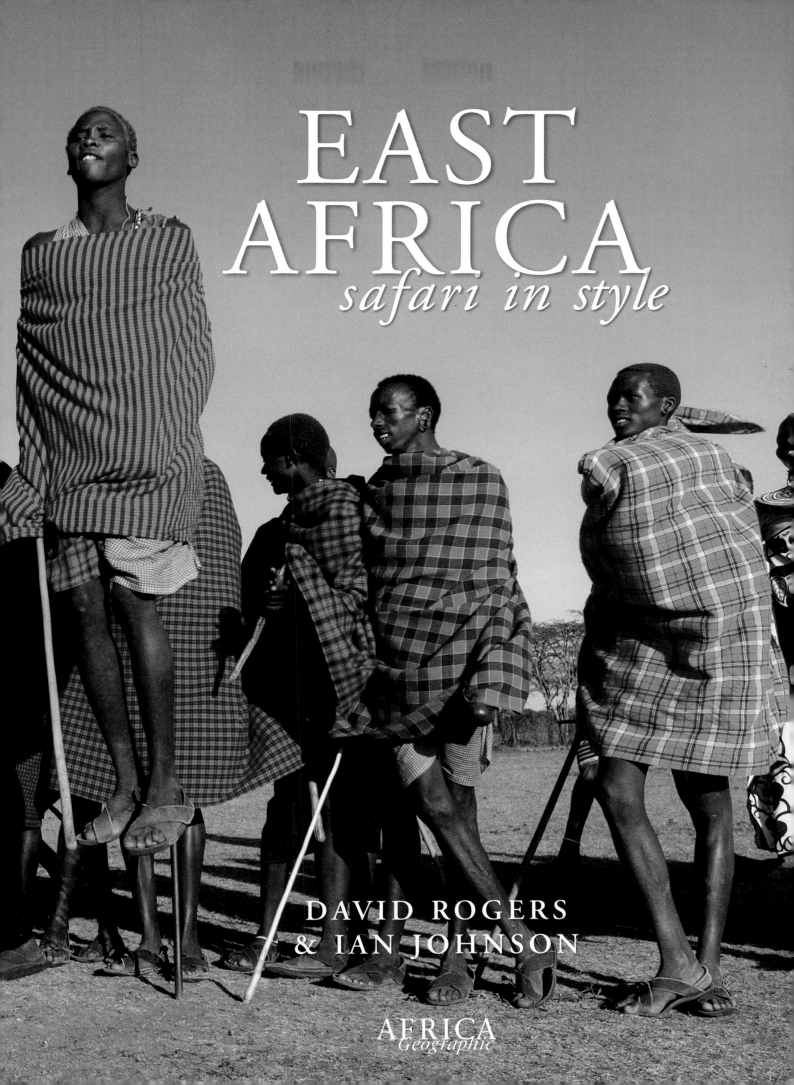

EAST
AFRICA
safari in style

DAVID ROGERS
& IAN JOHNSON

AFRICA
Geographic

Over 75 years ago, British Airways' forerunner, Imperial Airways, pioneered a scheduled airline service to East Africa, helping to open up the region to travellers from the United Kingdom, Europe and beyond.

Those early adventurers returned home with stories about wide-open spaces teeming with wildlife, majestic mountains that rose out of the savanna and the rich tapestry of local cultures.

Today, East Africa continues to provide unrivalled nature- and cultural-travel experiences, with hotels, safari lodges and camps providing excellent accommodation. In return, the region and its people receive enormous economic benefits from international travel. British Airways recognises these advantages, which is why we are proud to be associated with the publication of *East Africa – Safari in Style*. This beautiful book explores many of the wonders of this corner of Africa, providing an alluring glimpse of some of its wildlife, lodges, game reserves and national parks. It will, we hope, encourage you to pack your bags and to experience what is deservedly still considered one of Africa's prime destinations.

S. D Tyagi

Suneel Tyagi
British Airways General Manager, East Africa

BRITISH AIRWAYS

contents

UGANDA
KENYA
TANZANIA

introducing east africa

The word safari comes from the Kiswahili word for a journey and, for most people, a safari to East Africa is, indeed, the journey of a lifetime. Justifiably so, for this vast area straddling the equator is home to some of the richest wildlife areas in Africa. It also has spectacular landscapes that are quintessentially African, from snow-capped Mount Kilimanjaro, the limitless plains of the Serengeti and the wonder of Ngorongoro Crater in Tanzania to Uganda's glorious lakes and forested mountains and Kenya's game-rich wild areas. This is the place where some of Africa's first hominids walked and the forests are still filled with dozens of primates, including gorillas, chimps and innumerable monkeys.

East Africa – Safari in Style visits some of the finest game lodges, safari camps and hotels in this wedge of the continent, from the centrally located to the remote. Photojournalists David Rogers and Ian Johnson have undertaken a journey of their own to give you a personal insight into the activities and accommodation on offer.

With one-quarter of its land dedicated to conservation areas, Tanzania is the game-lover's dream. Here is the vast Serengeti National Park, probably the most famous game reserve in the world, renowned for its annual wildebeest migration and for the numerous predators that prowl in its wake. Tanzania has lots more to offer as well: some of the highest mountains in Africa (including Mount Kilimanjaro, the highest); Ngorongoro Crater, the world's largest intact volcanic caldera; a share of Lake Tanganyika, the second deepest freshwater lake on earth; a necklace of exotic islands and more than 25 other game sanctuaries.

Wildlife knows no political boundaries and the annual wildebeest migration moves from the Serengeti northwards, crossing the Mara River in spectacular, and well-documented, fashion to Kenya's Masai Mara National Reserve in search of fresh, rich grazing. Famous for national parks and reserves and dozens of private sanctuaries, Kenya is also a region of great scenic diversity, with its snow-topped Mount Kenya, northern wilderness areas, Great Rift Valley, Maasai heartlands and coral Indian Ocean coast.

To the west lies Uganda, with its dense montane rainforests and the primates that live in them. Uganda's safari experiences are rapidly becoming as sophisticated as those of its eastern neighbours, with luxury lodges offering intimate game-viewing and elegant accommodation. This is the place to see gorillas, chimpanzees and an abundance of monkeys in their natural habitat.

No introduction to East Africa would be complete without mentioning the people. In a continent known for its political upheavals and ethnic conflict, there are many who are committed to conservation and to improving the quality of life of all the continent's inhabitants. By visiting the safari destinations covered in this book, you'll be contributing both to their upliftment and the economic growth of the countries they call home.

the woodland belt
selous game reserve &
western tanzania

Acacias, baobabs and brachy-stegias dominate the *miombo* woodland that covers a broad swathe of southern and western Tanzania. These regions offer game-viewing in the raw, from Selous Game Reserve, the largest wildlife sanctuary in Africa, to the forested Mahale Mountains National Park, which lies on the shore of Lake Tanganyika and is best known for its habituated chimp communities.

Elephants, Katavi National Park, Tanzania

D. & S. BALFOUR/WWW.DARYLBALFOUR.COM

chada katavi
katavi national park

Katavi National Park is one of Tanzania's best-kept secrets. In its heart is Chada Katavi, a secluded camp offering magnificent game-viewing.

The drive to Chada Katavi from the grass airstrip should take no more than 20 minutes, but it is rare for the journey to take less than an hour as there is so much to see *en route*. My most recent visit was no different. We passed large herds of zebras and topis, dozens of giraffes, numerous elephants making their way down to the waterholes, hundreds of hippos dozing in a muddy wallow, a sizeable herd of roan antelope and several somnolent lions lazing in the shade of a sausage-tree.

With such abundant game, Katavi National Park should be teeming with visitors, but it is very remote and isolated and requires a lengthy charter flight from the country's more populous destinations. Proclaimed in 1974, it is, at 4 471 square kilometres, the third-largest national park in Tanzania, and is reputed to hold Africa's largest remaining buffalo herds. In addition, the country's highest density of crocodiles and hippos gather in the seasonally flooded Katavi and Chada lakes, and there are also healthy populations of other species, including major predators such as lions, leopards, hyaenas and wild dogs.

Probably the most intriguing creatures for me at Katavi are the giant crocodiles, leviathans that mass in huge clusters when the seasonal rivers dry up and spend much of the dry season lying up in caves they have excavated in the banks of the riverbed. To see 30 or more crocs lying intertwined in a cave, their cold eyes watching every movement you make, is quite enthralling… and chilling.

Chada Katavi camp is set in the midst of this untamed wilderness, and manages to keep its guests completely comfortable without detracting in any way from the sense of being in a truly wild area. Large custom-built tents, each with *en-suite* facilities and located far enough from its neighbours to ensure complete privacy, recreate the atmosphere of the expeditions of the early explorers, with kerosene lanterns for lighting and piping-hot bucket showers filled on demand. Meals are served with gleaming silverware in a homely mess tent or alfresco, and there's a comfortable library tent with an array of memorabilia, books and weathered maps, where evening drinks and snacks are served prior to dinner. Meals are a mouth-watering tribute to the chefs, whose ability to create extraordinary dishes so far from the nearest supermarket or delicatessen is astonishing.

Established by long-time Tanzanian safari pioneers Roland and Zoe Purcell, Chada Katavi maintains an atmosphere of being a home away from home. In fact, that is exactly what the camp is for the Purcells. This small, intimate camp has none of the finery of the super-stylish 'designer' lodges, but is instead a unique destination for wilderness enthusiasts in one of Africa's far-too-rapidly dwindling truly wild places. Just the way I like it.

PREVIOUS SPREAD Lions laze in the sun on the dusty grasslands of Katavi National Park.

THIS SPREAD Guided walking safaris will reveal a wealth of plains game.

A huddle of crocodiles in a cave.

Candlelit dinners can be taken in the mess tent, or alfresco, if preferred.

Hippos wallow in Lake Katavi.

Large tents, shaded by trees, recreate the atmosphere of the camps of early explorers.

NOMAD TANZANIA

To see 30 or more crocs lying intertwined in a cave... is quite enthralling... and chilling

PAUL JOYNSON-HICKS (3)

details

When to go
Chada Katavi is closed from mid-February to mid-May. The wet season is between March and May. October and November are the hottest months, although game-viewing is still good.

How to get there
Scheduled flights are available from Arusha on Monday and Thursday each week. It is also possible to charter a private flight from Dar es Salaam or Ruaha National Park. Katavi National Park is accessible by road from Mbeya in the south, but this is a full day's drive and fuel supplies are unreliable.

Who to contact
Nomad Tanzania owns and operates a number of safari camps throughout Tanzania. For more details, go to *www.nomad-tanzania. com*, or to *www.chada-katavi.com* for more information on Chada Katavi. Nomad Tanzania does not take direct bookings. Contact *info@nomad.co.tz* to find an agent in your area.

D. & S. BALFOUR/WWW.DARYLBALFOUR.COM

greystoke mahale

mahale mountains national park

Along the eastern shores of Lake Tanganyika, below a huge

tropical forest, is the tiny sanctuary of Greystoke Mahale, with

the world's largest known population of chimpanzees.

It's easy to imagine Tarzan swinging through the rich semi-tropical forest in the Mahale Mountains National Park, so it's fitting that the lodge that perches beneath lushly wooded slopes should bear the family name of this 'lord of the apes'.

Greystoke Mahale must be one of the most startlingly exotic destinations in Africa. Its main building, designed to resemble a Tongwe chief's hut, squats on the eastern shore of Lake Tanganyika, with the Mahale Mountains rising more than 2 500 metres at its back.

The lodge is the brainchild of Irish adventurer Roland Purcell, who stumbled upon the area while travelling through Africa in the 1980s. Here, on the spectacular site where he decided to settle and build a camp, is the very best of forest and beach. Roland has since joined forces with safari-camp operating company Nomad Tanzania, and they now run the lodge as a team.

The nearest road to the Mahale Mountains National Park is over 60 kilometres away, so it takes about six hours to reach from Arusha (four hours by air and two hours by boat). This inaccessibility conspires to make Mahale extraordinarily remote.

Your journey is rewarded with sensational accommodation in one of six secluded bandas set back in the forest. Each bedroom is open-fronted, and is equipped with furniture made of sun-bleached dhow wood, as well as chill-out decks. Walking down the narrow boardwalk through the forest to my bathroom, I half expected to find Robinson Crusoe stepping out of the shower.

Life feels easy at Mahale. We walked barefoot on the sand, wore swimming costumes and sarongs, and ate delicious meals, including fresh fish and home-made bread that would have satisfied the most discerning castaway. At night we were lulled to sleep by the gentle rush of waves washing up and down the beach.

Mahale has about 1 000 wild chimpanzees – and 60 or so that live in the forest near Greystoke Mahale. The latter have been studied by Japanese scientists from Kyoto University since 1965, and are now habituated.

We visited the forest in October at the end of the dry season, when the chimps spend most of their time on the lower slopes. Our guides Seif and his father Mohammed kept in contact with the Japanese researchers, so usually had a very good idea of where the chimps were at any given time. This made our trekking relatively easy and we were able to locate them on each foray into the forest. The chimps were so accustomed to humans that they were once spotted walking right through the camp. During wetter seasons, they take refuge deeper in the forest, and you'd be lucky to see them once or twice during a stay.

Lodge rules were strict about viewing protocol, with groups being limited to six people for just one hour a day. Nevertheless, we came to recognise the chimp family groups, the dominant males, the cute babies and the characters among them. I developed something of a connection with Darwin – a pale-faced, freckled young male who seemed to avoid all conflict and always appeared deep in thought.

Greystoke Mahale
must be one of the
most *startlingly exotic*
destinations in Africa

PREVIOUS SPREAD The lodge's main building has been designed to resemble a Tongwe chief's hut.

THIS SPREAD About 60 chimpanzees live in the forest near Greystoke Mahale.

On the sandy shores of Lake Tanganyika.

It is hard to resist the lure of a comfortable chair and a striking view.

Fine cuisine and chimp tales combine to make entertaining meal-times.

With their close evolutionary kinship to humans, chimps make fascinating study subjects.

Snorkelling in the lake reveals a treasure of freshwater life.

The bandas are tucked in a patch of woodland behind the beach.

Lanterns and a tranquil lake make the perfect dinner setting.

The forest is not only about chimps. Other primate species that make their home here include vervet and colobus monkeys, and there are also bushbuck, bushpig, leopard and an amazing variety of birds. The mountains, which stretch 50 kilometres from north to south, with an average height of 2 400 metres, are a meeting place of bird species from west and east Africa, with many showing closer similarities to the creatures of Rwanda, Uganda and Burundi than those of the Eastern Arc Mountains. Birds found here include red-chested sunbirds, blue-breasted bee-eaters, yellow-rumped tinkerbirds, African olive pigeons and tambourine doves. In the miombo woodlands are Retz's helmet-shrikes, orange-winged pytilia and black-backed barbets.

The lake itself is reason enough for visiting Mahale. Lake Tanganyika is 720 kilometres long, 70 kilometres wide and up to 1 440 metres deep (the second deepest in the world after Lake Baikal in Russia) and holds one sixth of the world's fresh water. The water is alkaline, with little algae growth, and as a result it is crystal clear. On still days it's like a mirror, but the wind can quickly whip up the surface into waves. It's possible to explore the lake by kayak or dhow.

The lake is rich in aquatic life, with about 260 species of endemic cichlids (pronounced *sicklids*), a freshwater form of jellyfish, water cobras, hippos and abundant birds. We went snorkelling in a quiet bay strewn with large boulders and found numerous cichlids, many of which are confined to this eastern corner of the lake. One species incubates eggs in its mouth; another keeps guard at its nest. My thrill was spotting a water cobra slipping away beneath a rock. These venomous snakes hunt fish, but are extremely shy of people.

Our hosts were a knowledgeable couple from England and Australia. Since then Doug Braum and Magdalena Lukasik-Braum, who both previously worked at the Centre for the Rehabilitation of Wildlife in Durban, South Africa, have taken over the lodge. Doug is a keen photographer who has worked throughout Africa; Magdalena is a vet who has worked at the Jane Goodall Institute in Gombe, Nigeria. Passionate about their new project, the Braums are sure to be fascinating hosts.

The water is alkaline, with little algae growth, and as a result it is *crystal clear*

details

When to go
The lodge is closed between mid-March and mid-May for routine maintenance.

How to get there
Greystoke Mahale is accessible twice-weekly on a four-hour flight from Arusha, then a two-hour boat ride on Lake Tanganyika.

Who to contact
Nomad Tanzania owns and operates a number of safari camps throughout Tanzania. For more details, go to *www.nomad-tanzania.com*, or *www.greystoke-mahale.com* for more information on Greystoke Mahale. Nomad Tanzania does not take direct bookings, but contact *info@nomad.co.tz* to find an agent in your area.

sand rivers selous

selous game reserve

Tucked into a remote corner of Selous Game Reserve

is a lodge so isolated you feel like you are the first person

to visit this remarkable wilderness area.

'**When I first began safaris in Selous** more than 20 years ago,' says Richard Bonham, 'I travelled the length of this amazing reserve, but I found myself returning again and again to the Sand Rivers area with its variety of terrains and ever-reliable game. When we finally decided to create Sand Rivers Selous, it was obvious where we should settle.' The lodge and its eight open-fronted chalets are positioned on a rocky outcrop above a sweep of the broad Rufiji River, with its sandbanks, hippos and rich birdlife, and a toehold in the largest conservation area in Africa.

Selous Game Reserve was named for the famed hunter Frederick Courtney Selous, who was shot by a German sniper not far from the site of the Sand Rivers lodge during World War I. The reserve extends across 55 000 square kilometres of untamed wilderness – it's larger than Denmark and is the second-largest protected natural area in the world. It also forms part of the Selous–Niassa transboundary ecosystem, which extends for 155 000 square kilometres across southern Tanzania and northern Mozambique.

In Selous, just 1 000 square kilometres north of the Rufiji River have been set aside for safaris. The Sand Rivers Selous lodge has a prime position in the remote southwestern part of this area and, despite our driving great distances each day, no other vehicles appeared to destroy the illusion that we were its first visitors.

'The great thing about Selous is that you can do something different every day,' said my local guide. 'We have the river, lakes, hot springs and bush, and we offer game drives, walking tours, boat cruises, fishing and fly-camping.' On our first morning we went boating up the Rufiji River, past hippos and crocodiles and through the ravine called Stiegler's Gorge, after a Swiss explorer killed in the area by an elephant in the early 1900s. Leopards are often spotted here. We saw a pack of rare wild dogs,

In the baking afternoon *we watched lazily* as large numbers of elephants and giraffes came to drink

PREVIOUS SPREAD The lodge overlooks the Rufiji River.

Each room is furnished with net-draped beds and local artefacts.

THIS SPREAD You can even watch for wildlife while having a delicious meal.

Selous Game Reserve has a healthy population of elephants.

A hippo family passes beneath the lodge.

Guides are armed to protect visitors.

The lodge's pool provides a cool end to a day spent in the African sun.

as well as African skimmers, African fish-eagles, kingfishers, egrets and storks.

One morning, we hiked past a series of beautiful lakes fed by the Sand River – Makubi, Segese and Tagalala (which holds the greatest concentration of crocodiles in Africa). We spotted palm-nut vultures, yellow-billed storks, white-crowned lapwings and bee-eaters, and shared our sightings over a sizzling breakfast of eggs and sausages prepared by our guide on an open fire. In the baking afternoon we watched lazily as large numbers of elephants and giraffes came to drink.

Black rhino were once plentiful in Selous, but poachers seeking to sell their horns have hunted them almost to extinction. The Selous Rhino Trust, established to address the rhino problem, has a base on the river and over the past 10 years has identified 16 black rhino in the region, which suggests that their numbers are recovering.

Sand Rivers Selous offers a sophisticated safari experience, with lavish lunches and candlelit three-course dinners. The thatched chalets each have a king-sized bed, *en-suite* bathroom and an air of plush yesteryear elegance.

I elected to spend one night fly-camping beside the shimmering waters of Lake Tagalala. We stayed in square tents made of mosquito netting, with separate tents for dressing, toilets and hot-water showers. Dinner was served at a table beneath the stars to the inimitable soundtrack of grunting hippos, roaring lions and whooping hyaenas.

details

When to go
Sand Rivers Selous is closed from mid-March to mid-May.

How to get there
There are daily flights to the lodge from Dar es Salaam, Zanzibar, Ruaha, Mafia, Pemba and northern Tanzania.

Who to contact
Nomad Tanzania owns and operates safari camps throughout Tanzania. For more details, go to *www.nomad-tanzania.com*, or *www.sand-rivers-selous. com* for more information on Sand Rivers Selous. Nomad Tanzania does not take direct bookings. Contact *info@nomad.co.tz* to find an agent in your area.

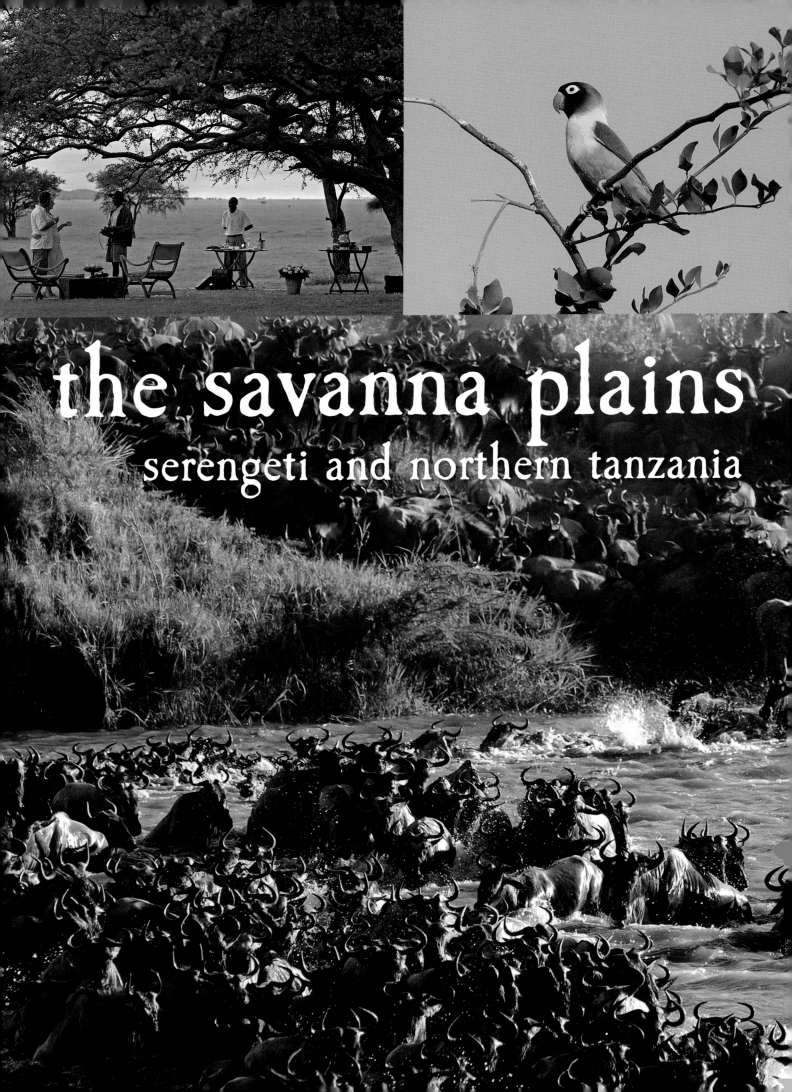

the savanna plains

serengeti and northern tanzania

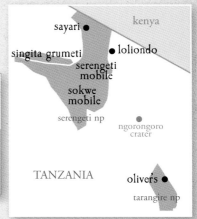

Tanzania's northern safari circuit embraces some of Africa's best-known wildlife areas. The grassland plains of the Serengeti National Park, together with Kenya's Masai Mara, are famously associated with surging herds of wildebeest on their never-ending migration cycle as they follow the rains and good grazing. To the east is Ngorongoro Crater, probably the best place in East Africa to see black rhino, while baobab-strewn Tarangire comes into its own during the dry winter months, when elephants congregate along the Tarangire River.

Wildebeest crossing the Mara River, Serengeti National Park, Tanzania

sayari
singita grumeti
loliondo
serengeti mobile
sokwe mobile
serengeti np
ngorongoro crater
kenya
uganda
kenya
tanzania
TANZANIA
oliver's
tarangire np

The Nomad Tanzania mobile camps follow the wildebeest migration, ensuring that visitors miss none of the wildlife action.

loliondo & serengeti mobile camps
greater serengeti

Hyaena laughter cut through the night. Jackals were also on the move and a lone lion boomed from the boundary of its territory. It was early February in the Serengeti. Wildebeest by the million – and their attendant predators – were gathering on the short-grass plains. And, true to form, Nomad Tanzania (which also runs the permanent camps Chada Katavi in Katavi National Park, Greystoke Mahale in Mahale Mountains National Park and Sand Rivers Selous in the Selous Game Reserve) had positioned their mobile camp in the midst of the action.

I had arrived at the camp earlier in the day, tired and dusty, to find a hot shower (delivered by bucket from the fire), cold white wine, a roaring campfire and friendly hosts. This was an experience in the true safari tradition, with four luxury *en-suite* tents a stroll away from the candlelit mess tent. Nomad Tanzania has a private vehicle and driver for every group, but in camp travellers gathered to exchange wildlife notes. One group had seen a leopard in a tree, another the elusive striped hyaena.

Nomad Tanzania's mobile camps include Serengeti Safari Camp and Loliondo Safari Camp, whose only difference is that the first moves within the park, shadowing the wildebeest migration, while the Loliondo camp moves seasonally within Maasai community areas along the Serengeti's eastern border.

'People often talk of "normal migrations",' said Nomad's chief guide Richard Knocker. 'But in our experience there is no such thing as a normal migration. We stay as mobile as possible and can move the camp every two weeks to give people the best chance to see the action.'

During the wet season, Serengeti Safari Camp stays with the migration in the southern Ndutu region, where the wildebeest calve and predators abound. May and June is rutting season, when impossibly long lines of migrating wildebeest move north to Moru Kopjes and the Western Corridor. The camp accompanies them and by June or early July is well positioned to watch the herds gathering on the bank of the Grumeti River. From mid-July through to November, the wildebeest concentrate close to the Mara and Bologonja rivers. High drama invariably unfolds when the animals eventually cross the croc-infested waters.

When I arrived, the Loliondo camp was located in its wet-season location in the Piyaya Village region bordering the Serengeti Park, Ngorongoro Conservation Area and the Gol Mountains. The plains were alive with game.

The dry season, from mid-June to November, sees the animals move northwards. In their wake is the camp, which then partners with Ololosokwan Village in the northern Loliondo area bordering Kenya's Masai Mara National Reserve and the Serengeti. The advantage of being outside the parks is that you can enjoy night drives, walking tours and Maasai visits, which are not available within the park. You are also contributing to the support of the local communities. 'During the 2005/6 seasons, Nomad Tanzania contributed US$38 000 to the Ololosokwan area and US$22 000 to the Piyaya area,' said Richard. 'The money was spent on health care for the poor of the area and school fees for 74 kids. This is a classic example of tourism helping both a culture and its immediate environment – with small, well-targeted initiatives that bring tangible benefits to entire communities.'

PREVIOUS SPREAD Evenings at the campfire are illuminated by lanterns.

Getting up close and personal to the game.

THIS SPREAD Ostriches are plentiful in the Serengeti-Mara ecosystem.

The heart of the camp is the open fire – the perfect spot around which to share safari tales.

Breakfast on the plains.

Wildebeest cover the open plains in the Piyaya area.

Wildebeest by the million – *and their attendant predators* – were gathering on the short-grass plains

details

When to go
The camps are open all year.

How to get there
Fly into Serengeti or Loliondo and your private game-viewing vehicle will be waiting on the strip. Daily flights link these camps with Nomad's sister camp in Tarangire National Park, Nomad Tarangire.

Who to contact
Nomad Tanzania owns and operates a number of mobile camps throughout Tanzania. For more details, go to *www.nomad-tanzania.com*, or to *www.serengeti-safari-camp.com* for more information on their Serengeti and Loliondo mobile camps. Nomad Tanzania does not take direct bookings, so contact *info@nomad.co.tz* to find an agent in your area.

oliver's camp
tarangire national park

Walking tours are the speciality of this exciting camp, which is situated in a reserve that, despite its small size, supports an impressive collection of wild animals.

The roar of a male lion defining his territory is a pretty humbling experience at the best of times. When you're in a fly tent with walls so thin you can see the stars through the fabric, it's mind-blowing. Lying in the darkness listening to the sounds of the African night, I figured that this was precisely the sort of experience that naturalist and guide Paul Oliver had in mind when he set up Oliver's Camp in the wilderness area of Tanzania's Tarangire National Park.

UK-born Oliver fell in love with Tanzania in the 1980s while exploring Africa, and set up a bush home in a Maasai-owned concession on the outskirts of Tarangire. From this site, he conducted walking trails into the park. In 2001, Tanzania National Parks allowed him to set up camp within Tarangire's boundaries. Now, in addition to the walks (they last from one hour to four days), guests can take open-vehicle game drives.

Fly-camping in the wilderness with nothing between you and nature but a three-metre-square tent of heavy-duty mosquito netting may not be everyone's cup of tea, even though guests are provided with comfortable bedding, hot showers

and fine cuisine. If you're hesitant, opt for Oliver's base camp, where you can unwind in one of eight exquisitely appointed guest tents so generously spaced that you can sit on your veranda and look across the koppie-studded Tarangire Plains and feel thoroughly alone.

Swallowed up by a comfortable armchair in the library tent, I explored the impressive collection of natural-history books, seedpods, skulls, maps and other curiosities. Drinks and coffee can be arranged in a snap, so it's easy to spend hours here learning about the country, its history and its animals, or simply chilling out. My reverie was broken only by the whydahs, silverbills and finches that fluttered constantly at the birdbath outside.

At the end of the day, the guests gathered around the stone fireplace beside the dining tent, sipping drinks, absorbing the view of the dense stands of palms and thick acacia forest around the camp, and sharing the day's sightings.

At 2 600 square kilometres, Tarangire is one of Tanzania's smaller national parks, but it forms part of a far larger ecosystem. Much of it

consists of open savanna plains dotted with baobabs, apart from the permanent water of the Tarangire River and the Silale Swamp area in the south. It is to these wet places that, during the dry season, hundreds of elephants and large herds of wildebeest, zebra and many other species converge. In their wake come the big cats.

The park also embraces the western limits of the Somali-Maasai biome, home to fringe-eared oryx, gerenuk and striped hyaena, among many others. Bird species number some 550 – a tally than tops both Serengeti National Park and Ngorongoro Conservation Area.

Guides Albert Lucas and Peter Tetlow led me on foot along dry *karongos* (gullies) to springs that have broken through the ground to form waterholes. Here we saw signs of the lions, elephants and buffalo that come to drink during the dry season. In 2005, Oliver's was incorporated into Asilia Lodges and Camps (Asilia also manages Sayari, Olakira and Suyan camps in the Serengeti ecosystem and Matemwe Bungalows on Zanzibar, and the group operates mobile camps throughout Tanzania).

OLIVER'S CAMP

PREVIOUS SPREAD Fly-camping provides a unique opportunity to experience the sounds of an African night.

Elephants at Tarangire National Park. During the dry season, they congregate in great numbers along the Tarangire River.

THIS SPREAD Guests stretch their legs and have a welcome cup of tea beneath a giant sausage-tree.

Oliver's base camp offers luxury accommodation and attentive service.

The martial eagle is frequently spotted in savanna environments.

Dinners combine excellent cuisine and the finest wines.

My reverie was broken only by the whydahs, silverbills and finches that *fluttered constantly at the birdbath* outside

details

When to go
Game-viewing is best during the dry season, from June to March.

How to get there
Tarangire is two hours by road from Arusha. From the park gate it is two-hour drive to the camp. There is an airstrip 45 minutes away, with daily connections to other safari destinations.

Who to contact
Tel. (+255-27) 250 4118 or (+255-74) 876 3338, fax (+255-27) 250 2799. E-mail *oliverscamp@asilialodges.com* or go to *www.asilialodges.com*

sayari camp
greater serengeti

Perfectly poised to watch the wildebeest plunging

across the Mara River, Sayari Camp also offers

excellent accommodation and fine cuisine.

The migration of three million ungulates across the 15 000-square-kilometre Serengeti National Park is the greatest wildlife show on earth – and also one of the most popular.

The central region of the park has seen an increase in tourist camps and can be overcrowded. If you'd like your view of the migrating herds to be less populous, Sayari Camp is your best bet. Here, in the remote, seldom-visited Mara River region in the north-west, bordering Kenya's Masai Mara National Reserve, Asilia Lodges and Camps has set up a stylish tented camp.

The animal viewing is good too. After spending the wet season on the short-grass Serengeti plains, the wildebeest herds move northwards, reaching the Mara River between July and November. Thousands of visitors flock to the Masai Mara each year to witness this migration, unaware that most of the action actually occurs on the Tanzanian side of the border.

Sayari Camp is perfectly positioned to see the animals crossing the river and you can wait in comfort while numbers build up on the banks. Once the first wildebeest plunges into the water, the rest follow in a spectacle that can go on for hours and produces exceptional photographic opportunities. Wildebeest are perfectly designed for covering long distances, but they are less comfortable in water and many fall prey to the massive crocodiles that lie in wait.

The camp's large camel-coloured tents are set up beneath trees just a few hundred metres from the river. Each has a king-sized bed, a private veranda with comfortable seating, and an *en-suite* bathroom with a shower, 'his' and 'hers' vanity basins, flush toilets and hot running water delivered via a hidden bucket system. Two central tents house a dining room and a lounge with leather and chrome furniture. We gathered on the sofas before game drives and meals, but the cool evenings drew us to the fire outside, where we drank red wine and watched the stars move in and the owls hoot their watch.

Outside the migration season there is still plenty of action. Large pods of hippos and huge crocodiles remain resident in the Mara River and herds of topi and eland take over the plains, sharing the land with lions, cheetahs, elephants, hyaenas, bat-eared foxes and honey badgers. In a massive, acacia-dotted plain known as the Wedge, a scattering of permanent spring-fed pools attract antelope by the thousands. We saw topi, eland, Thomson's gazelle, impala, red hartebeest and wildebeest, not to mention zebra, hyaenas, a giraffe family, crowned cranes, a cheetah we flushed out of the grass and two fat male lions lounging beneath a spindly tree. In the distance, the escarpment demarcated the border with Kenya, and around us the abundant wildlife and sheer magnificence of the Serengeti were overwhelming. And there was not another vehicle in sight.

Asilia Lodges and Camps has excellent coverage of the greater Serengeti area. The luxury mobile Olakira Camp travels between the southern and central Serengeti areas, staying close to large concentrations of animals while skirting the tourist spots. Suyan Camp operates in the wild Loliondo area, bordering Serengeti on the east. The concession areas offer privileges not available in the park, such as walking safaris, night drives and Maasai cultural activities. The group also offers mobile camping throughout Tanzania and operates Oliver's Camp in Tarangire National Park and Matemwe Bungalows on Zanzibar.

SAYARI CAMP

cool evenings drew us to the fire outside, where we *drank red wine* and watched the stars

PREVIOUS SPREAD Evening meals are often served outdoors, with lighting provided by lanterns and the starry African sky.

Cheetahs are regularly seen on the Serengeti grasslands.

THIS SPREAD Sayari's tents nestle beneath trees overlooking the Mara River.

Lions are most often seen on the grassy plains or basking on a rock.

Dinner in the wilderness.

Friendly service and outstanding cuisine.

Tents have king-sized beds and *en-suite* bathroom facilities.

SAYARI CAMP

details

When to go
The camp is open all year except during the long rains between mid-April and May. The migration typically visits the Mara River area from mid-July to mid-November, but it is hard to predict the animal movements accurately.

How to get there
The camp can be reached by air or safari vehicle.

Who to contact
Tel. (+255-27) 250 4118/9, or (+255-784) 76 3338, e-mail *sayaricamp@asilialodges.com* or go to *www.asilialodges.com*

singita grumeti
reserves

serengeti national park

Cutting a swathe across the Serengeti's Western Corridor, Grumeti

Reserves offers prolific game-viewing in an area rarely visited by man.

The 4x4 wound its way up a curved rocky path. Beneath us, the wild, sun-washed vastness of the Serengeti plains stretched to the horizon. As we crested the top of the hill, the colonial-style lodge with its deep, shady veranda came into view. Seven cottages were spread across the summit, each promising a private and exceptional view across the plains. This is Sasakwa Lodge, one of the most luxurious safari camps in the Serengeti National Park.

The lodge is one of three camps in the Singita Grumeti Reserves, a 141 000-hectare sweep across the northern section of Serengeti National Park's Western Corridor. Here there are no fences; it's a place of endless vistas, trees, hills and space. Of the camps, Sasakwa Lodge is definitely the grandest. Its cottages are named after adventure heroes such as Ernest Hemingway. There are numerous communal sitting rooms, as well as an extensive library, card and billiard rooms and retreats for watching TV. All are decorated with original wildlife masterpieces. My cottage, like the others, featured a king-sized bed, a sitting room, huge bathroom, private deck and heated swimming pool. The excellent sound system charmed me too, and I could see it would be difficult to leave. But the Serengeti is perhaps the most abundant ecosystem in the world, and I was soon lured out of my room by elephants crossing to a waterhole and great herds of antelope and zebra.

I was soon *lured out of my room* by elephants crossing to a waterhole and great herds of antelope and zebra

PREVIOUS SPREAD Mountain-biking is an excellent way to view plains game at Singita Grumeti, but an armed guard is necessary.

THIS SPREAD Dinners at Sasakwa Lodge combine fine food and endless vistas.

You can get really close to nature by exploring the plains on horseback.

Perched on a hill, Sasakwa Lodge offers panoramic views of the plains.

The spacious bedrooms recall the elegance of a bygone era.

A real treat – a massage with a view.

The marquee-shaped tents at Sabora Plains Tented Camp are roomy and comfortable.

Guides show visitors the best way to approach the animals.

Antique furniture and Persian rugs contrast with the wildness of the African plains outside.

A picnic breakfast served beneath a tree at Sabora.

Sabora camp at night.

My next stop was Sabora Plains Tented Camp, about 20 kilometres south-west of Sasakwa. As we arrived, I rubbed my eyes in disbelief – the camp was surrounded by impossibly manicured green lawns and trimmed balanites trees. The guide laughed at my surprise and explained, 'The gardeners here are the animals. The giraffes nibble the trees into shape, and the wild herbivores trim the lawns.' And the perfection extends to the accommodation. The camp may be a tented one, but no luxury has been spared. The six tents are lavishly outfitted with silk curtains, colonial and antique furniture, Persian rugs, air-conditioning and artefacts collected from all over East Africa.

The third camp, Faru Faru River Lodge, lies to the east of Sabora. Its style is a Tarzan-like modern interpretation of the traditional Maasai home. Six tented suites have been built beneath sycamore trees on a small hill overlooking a waterhole and the Grumeti River. In the dry season, animals come to drink and graze on the river vegetation. In places beneath the camp where the river has run dry, elephants dig waterholes, and from one of the viewing decks I watched buffalo, giraffes, zebras and topis came to drink. Later, while wallowing in the rock horizon pool, I watched as black-and-white colobus monkeys swung through the trees on the river banks. The Serengeti was once home to many black rhinos. Today fewer than 70 remain, and plans are afoot to re-introduce these great beasts to the Grumeti Reserves in the next few years.

'The gardeners here are the animals. The *giraffes nibble the trees* into shape, and the wild herbivores trim the lawns'

All the lodges are managed by the world-renowned Singita group of eco-tourism properties, and guests are encouraged to travel between the three for a comprehensive experience of the region and its wildlife. With the largest of these lodges accommodating just 28 guests, you're ensured silence and privacy.

When you're relaxing between wildlife walks and game drives, you can go horseback game-viewing or hot-air ballooning, play tennis or lawn croquet or ride mountain bikes.

At night, star-gazers can enjoy the studded African sky. Hedonistically, I tripped off to the fully equipped health spa for a relaxing aromatherapy massage. Later, with my muscles pummelled and coaxed into jelly-like submission, I reported to the sitting room for pre-dinner drinks, followed by a silver-serviced, candlelit dinner. I went to bed replete and, to the roar of a distant leopard, slipped into sleep.

At Faru Faru River Lodge, you can even watch the game from your bath.

The rock pool and deck at Faru Faru – the scene of lazy afternoons and sundowners.

Dine in style beneath a shady deck with your personal waiter in attendance.

The guides at Singita Grumeti Reserves are expert trackers. Here, footprints on the riverbank are explained.

At night, star-gazers can enjoy the *studded African sky*

details

When to go
Singita Grumeti Reserves is closed in April and May. March is the hottest month, July and August bring pleasantly cool mornings and evenings. Game-viewing is good throughout the year, although the best migration game-viewing is between May and August.

How to get there
Flights from Nairobi airport and Dar es Salaam land at Kilimanjaro International Airport, where a charter flight takes visitors to Grumeti. The reserve's airstrip is also served twice daily from Arusha.

Who to contact
For reservations, tel. (+27-21) 683 3424 or (+255-28) 262 2074 or (+1-770) 947 7049, e-mail *reservations@singita.co.za* or *reservations@grumetireserves.com*. Go to *www.grumetireserves.com* or *www.singita.com*

Sokwe Mobile Camps conduct most of their activities in community-owned areas far from the crush of the busy tourist routes.

sokwe mobile camps
greater serengeti

PREVIOUS SPREAD Portable washing facilities in the great outdoors.

Balloon rides offer unique views across the plains.

THIS SPREAD Sokwe offers comfortable tents, cold beer and attentive staff.

The Serengeti is home to a rich population of lions.

Maasai men display a traditional dance.

There's nothing like a hot, cooked meal after a few hours on the grasslands.

The secretarybird is common in the savanna and open grasslands.

The three camel-coloured safari tents, framed by a grove of exquisite flowering acacias, lured us with views towards the Serengeti National Park and the Mara River. Wide smiles greeted us as we clambered from our custom-built safari vehicle. Lunch was on the table, chilled wine was in the cooler and a team of people was standing by. After the long drive to the remote Loliondo area in the north-eastern Serengeti ecosystem, it was a wonderful reception – and all the more special in that the camp had been set up especially for us.

This sort of personalised approach is old hat to Sokwe, which has been offering mobile safari services to freelance professional guides in Tanzania since 1989. Its owners, whose wealth of knowledge covers everything from the seasons and climate to the movement patterns of game, also cater to film crews and private groups.

The site of this particular camp is very close to the border with Kenya. In the distance I could see the slopes of the Lobo Hills, the highest point of the Serengeti. These mountains lord over granite domes and rolling grasslands, known for their large prides of lions.

Sokwe Mobile Camps generally avoid popular tourist routes and conduct most of their activities in communal areas outside the park. In the Loliondo area, the company has been working with the Maasai in Ololosokwan village for more than a decade. The Maasai have established camp-sites for use by tour operators; in exchange they receive funds for school buildings and medical clinics, among other necessities. On our visit, word spread through the village that we were interested in viewing a local dance, and at sunset a group of 50 Maasai men and women jumped, danced, posed and paraded for our pleasure. Sokwe also encourages the Maasai, who are traditionally cattle herders, to safeguard local wildlife. With the full line-up found in neighbouring Serengeti, including elephant, buffalo, lion, leopard, cheetah and wild dog, there is plenty to protect.

I was impressed by the thoughtful inventiveness of my tent. It had wall-to-wall carpets, comfortable beds and wide windows to let in the breeze. There were cunning bedside canvas pockets so you could reach for your torch or water bottle at night with no risk of knocking it over. The tent had three defined compartments, with the sleeping area in the front, a dressing room behind it, and a toilet and shower at the rear. Each morning I was woken with a gentle whisper from the camp attendant outside my tent, followed by the welcome sounds of my basins being filled with hot water. After returning from an evening game drive, my bucket shower would be filled with water from the fire.

Our Sokwe team, *Ndlovu*, whose signature elephant motif decorated the centre of the dining table, were wonderful hosts. On the first day we sat down to sumptuous chicken Elizabeth, rice salad with cashew nuts and, for dessert, watermelon drizzled with honey. It would have left even royalty crying out for more.

details

When to go
The camps are mobile and follow the plains action all year.

How to get there
International flights land at Kilimanjaro International Airport. Sokwe will meet visitors and also arranges internal flights on either scheduled or private charters.

Who to contact
Tel. (+255-27) 250 4118/9 or (+255-74) 899 9735, e-mail *sales@sokwe.com* or visit *www.sokwe.com* or *www.asilialodges.com*

mountains of the
arusha, meru & mount kilimanjaro

rift valley

Arusha is Tanzania's bustling safari capital, offering accommodation to many visitors *en route* to game reserves and wilderness areas. Nearby are Mount Meru, Africa's fifth highest peak, and majestic Mount Kilimanjaro, soaring more than five kilometres above the plains. Both were formed by the same volcanic activity that created the geologically dramatic Great Rift Valley 15 to 20 million years ago.

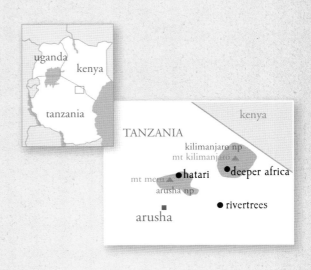

Mount Kilimanjaro, Tanzania

deeper africa
mount kilimanjaro

Africa's highest mountain offers snowy peaks and limitless views. There are various routes to the summit, from the physically demanding to gentler, less populous paths for novices and those who want to take in the scenery.

PREVIOUS SPREAD Mount Kilimanjaro from flamingo-filled
Momella Lakes.

A successful end to a day's climb.

THIS SPREAD An early-morning wake-up call with hot tea.

Giant senecios (*Senecio kilimanjari*).

A Deeper Africa guide and climbers tackle the slopes.

A night under the stars in a well-insulated tent.

Teatime, complete with tablecloth and piping-hot beverages.

Sipping a cup of piping hot coffee, I faced Kilimanjaro's Western Breach. The sun's last rays caressed its snowy peak, then slipped behind it, and the temperature started to plummet. I had completed my third day on the mountain, having overnighted first at Forest Camp and then at Shira, and reached Fischer Camp late in the afternoon. I'd enjoyed three superb hot meals every day, along with plenty of snacks, energy foods and filtered water. Some 3 962 metres below us lay the start of our climb, with the peak almost 2 000 metres above us. Yet I felt invigorated, with no signs of altitude sickness. Was it the good food, the comfortable, roomy tents, the expert advice from the guides or the crisp, unpolluted air on the mountain?

Kilimanjaro, the highest free-standing mountain in the world, lies on intersecting tectonic lines 80 kilometres east of the Great Rift Valley. The activity which created this volcano dates back less than a million years and the central ash-pit on Mount Kibo, its highest volcanic centre, may be only several hundred years old. Steam and sulphur fumaroles here indicate that the earth still stirs and heaves beneath the surface. Other volcanic peaks are Shira and Mawenzi, both of which are inactive. Shira peak collapsed about half a million years ago, leaving Shira Ridge as part of its caldera rim, while Mawenzi has been heavily eroded into a dramatic mass of steep-sided ridges and summits. Mount Kibo has three concentric craters, with the rim of the outermost crater rising to Uhuru Point – the chief summit at the 'top of the world'. Reusch, Kibo's central crater, contains the main fumaroles and, at its heart, a 130-metre-deep, 400-metre-wide ash pit. The outer crater has been breached by lava flows in several places. The most dramatic of these is the Western Breach, now outlined starkly against a darkening sky.

I had arranged my climb with the safari operator Deeper Africa, whose main focus is the safety and wellbeing of its clients. Before our ascent, we'd spent two days in Arusha National Park to overcome jetlag and acclimatise to the altitude while helping with preparations for the climb.

Deeper Africa offers various routes up Kilimanjaro but, wanting to avoid the more popular ascents, such as the five-day Marangu Route, I'd opted to try the Shira Plateau Route, a seven-day, gradual ascent that offers isolation and uninterrupted scenery. It also virtually guaranteed a successful climb. 'We've led climbers between the ages of 15 to 78 up this route,' said one of our guides, 'and 98 per cent of them made it to the summit.' Our two guides each had more than 100 climbs to their credit. They are all certified Wilderness First Responders, with extensive training in mountain medical emergencies and rescue procedures. I felt in safe hands.

Some 3 962 metres below us lay the start of our climb, with the peak almost 2 000 metres above us

details

When to go
You can climb Mount Kilimanjaro at any time of year, but take the climatic conditions into consideration. Be prepared for the cold and, in the rainy season, take waterproof clothing and equipment. March and September are the best seasons.

How to get there
Regular scheduled flights connect Dar es Salaam and Zanzibar to Kilimanjaro International Airport.

Who to contact
E-mail *info@deeperafrica.com* or go to *www.deeperafrica.com*

From the airport at Arusha, it's an hour by road through the dramatic Arusha National Park to Hatari, where abundant wildlife and diverse scenery combine with a soupçon of Hollywood glamour.

hatari lodge
arusha national park

A young couple, smiling beneath wide-brimmed cowboy hats, climbed out of their sunshine-orange Mercedes Benz 4x4 and came across to meet me. They introduced themselves as Jörg and Marlies Gabriel, the owners of Hatari Lodge. Within seconds it became evident that I was in for a thoroughly original and upbeat safari experience, for the lodge they run is sited on a Tanzanian farm with a history as charismatic as the personalities of its new caretakers.

Hatari Lodge, located at the northern entrance to Arusha National Park, encompasses kaleidoscopic landscapes, from the tallest mountains in Africa to craters, flamingo-filled lakes, its own Little Serengeti, and savanna plains that stretch north to Mount Kilimanjaro and Kenya's Amboseli National Park.

Its history is star-studded. The estate was originally the home of the German Margarete Trappe, who arrived from the coast by ox-wagon in 1907 and set down roots on a farm she named Momella, on the picturesque Meru Pass. In the 1960s' her son sold part of the farm to Hollywood's Paramount Pictures as the location for the John Wayne and Hardy Krüger movie *Hatari!*, about a pair of swashbuckling adventurers who capture wild animals for zoos. After the movie was released, Krüger purchased the farm in realisation of a lifelong dream to live in Africa, and stayed there for 13 years. Now, 30 years later, 'we are inviting people back,' says Marlies.

The lodge is certainly unique. Furnished in retro 1960s and '70s style, it combines moulded plastic seating and fibreglass tables inlaid with photographs of Hollywood celebrities, animal trophies made of goatskin that glow in the dark, bedrooms decorated with psychedelic wall murals and, in the saloon, a picture of 'Big John' presiding over the proceedings. Sisal carpets, a banana-bark roof and a lush, thoroughly African environment remind you where you are. So do mealtimes, which are sometimes held alfresco in the park or on a deck that juts out over the grassy plain in front of the lodge, where you may be closely observed by giraffes.

South of Hatari looms 4 566-metre Mount Meru, the fifth highest peak in Africa, while to the north is snow-capped Mount Kilimanjaro. In the orange Mercedes Benz Gelandewagen we explored the Momella Lakes with their large flocks of flamingos and pelicans, and negotiated a forested pass beneath chattering black-and-white colobus monkeys to the top of the Ngurdoto Crater. From the rim we looked down into its breathtaking three-kilometre-wide, 400-metre-deep volcanic cavity, on the floor of which grazing buffalo resembled slow-moving ants. Another attraction is Little Serengeti – an acacia-dotted grassland that attracts large herds of giraffe, zebra, wildebeest and buffalo. With more time, I could have canoed on the lakes, explored rainforests and even fly-camped at the base of Mount Kilimanjaro, where Maasai herders and their cattle live alongside big game, including tuskers, which are said to retire to these dusty, arid plains to die.

On our last evening we watched John Wayne and Hardy Krüger in supercool sunglasses and leather caps tearing across the Momella grassland in pursuit of a galloping black rhino. It was not your typical big-five safari experience – but, boy, was it fun!

mealtimes are sometimes held alfresco in the park or on a *deck that juts out over the grassy plain* in front of the lodge

details

When to go
Hatari lodge is open all year.

How to get there
The lodge is approximately one hour by road from Arusha International Airport.

Who to contact
E-mail *marlies@theafricanembassy.com* or go to *www.hatarilodge.com*

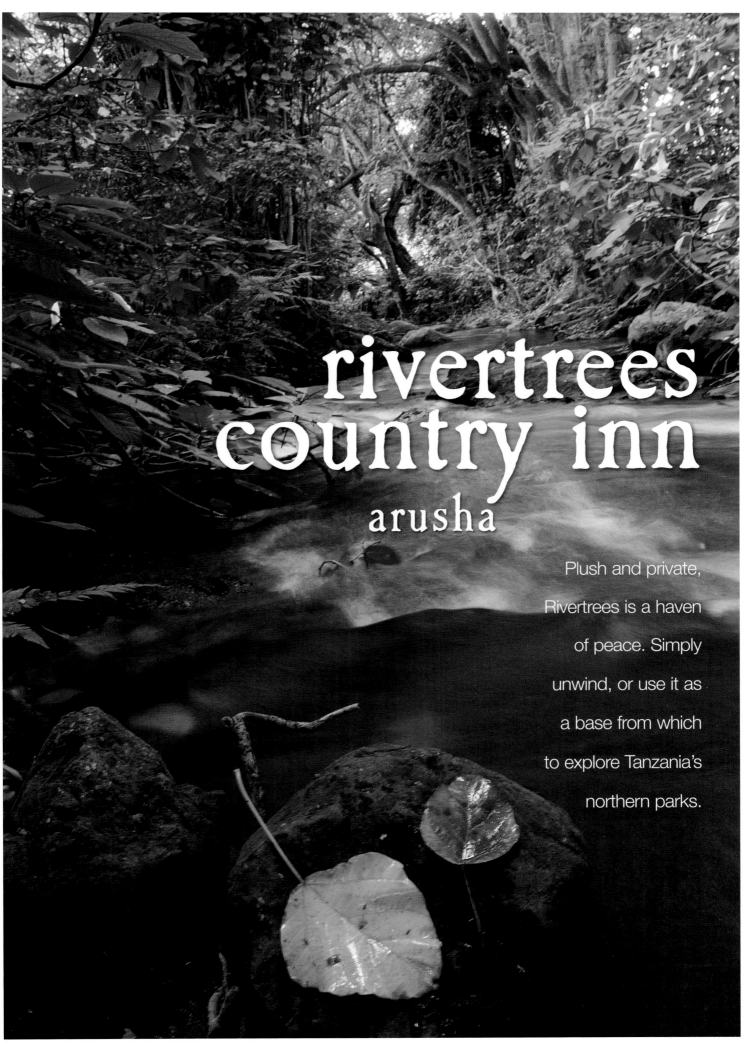

rivertrees
country inn
arusha

Plush and private,
Rivertrees is a haven
of peace. Simply
unwind, or use it as
a base from which
to explore Tanzania's
northern parks.

At the *foot of the garden* the gurgling Usa River flows fresh from Mount Meru to the north

Rivertrees Country Inn nestles in a lush, quiet setting outside the safari town of Arusha, with spectacular views of towering Mount Meru on one side and snow-capped Kilimanjaro on the other. Formerly a coffee plantation, the property is now a garden estate with massive pink, purple and mauve bougainvilleas, flame trees, strelitzias and manicured lawns. At the foot of the garden the gurgling Usa River flows fresh from Mount Meru to the north.

The inn feels more like a home than a hotel and accommodates just 28 guests who stay in self-contained suites, either in the main farmhouse or in the garden. I was shown to River House, tucked beneath tall trees on the riverbank. It had two *en-suite* bedrooms, a double-volume sitting room, a wood-burning fireplace, a kitchen, satellite television, a sound system and even its own broadband computer link. Each room has its own particular charm and is decorated with cherished old pictures, valuable books and original objects. There were kelims from the Orient, tea scales, old lamps, rugs, generous fabrics, antique glassware and lots of tin buckets filled with flowers.

History unfolds here too. At the bar, tucked between the open-sided kitchen and the dining room, I discovered an old recipe book, painstakingly penned by one of the property's original owners in 1926. On a wall, the same feisty matriarch is shown puffing a cigar with a safari guest in the 1930s. Another picture shows her standing beside a wood-sided truck laden with safari supplies on the slopes of Mount Meru. I also catch a glimpse of her grandson Richard as a young boy, proudly striking a pose with John Wayne when the Hollywood cowboy came to Arusha for the filming of *Hatari* in the early 1960s.

Arusha is a gateway to Tanzania's game parks and many other attractions. At 1 150 metres, many people also spend time here acclimatising to the altitude before climbing Mount Kilimanjaro. The inn is a short drive from Arusha National Park, which has fabulous high-altitude walks on the slopes of Mount Meru (4 565 metres). These are much quieter and no less impressive than those on Kilimanjaro.

A highlight of the park is the three-kilometre-wide volcanic Ngurdoto Crater, the lush floor of which is home to a small herd of buffalo. Also worth seeing are the alkaline Momella Lakes in the north-eastern sector of the park. Each lake is a different shade, dictated by the dominant mineral in the water. The lakes offer some of the best waterbird-viewing in Tanzania, with flocks of flamingos, pelicans, little grebes and waders.

At Rivertrees, horse rides and golf outings can be arranged, or you can take a trip to one of the local coffee plantations, or shop till you drop at the local markets or in Arusha.

PREVIOUS SPREAD Rivertrees Country Inn is the perfect base from which to explore the northerly parks of Tanzania.

The Usa River tumbles along the foot of the garden.

THIS SPREAD Each bedroom has been given its own character. Here rustic furniture combines with traditional pieces.

Locally grown fresh produce is brought to the inn daily.

Rivertrees Country Inn at night.

A relaxed meal beneath the trees.

There are comfortable corners for chatting, reading or relaxing throughout the inn.

details

When to go
Rivertrees is closed in April, but is open for the rest of the year.

How to get there
Rivertrees is situated roughly midway between Kilimanjaro International Airport and Arusha, about 20 minutes by road from each.

Who to contact
Tel. (+255-27) 255 3894, fax (+255-27) 255 3893, cell (+255-173) 33 9873. E-mail *rivertrees@habari.co.tz* or go to *www.rivertrees.com*

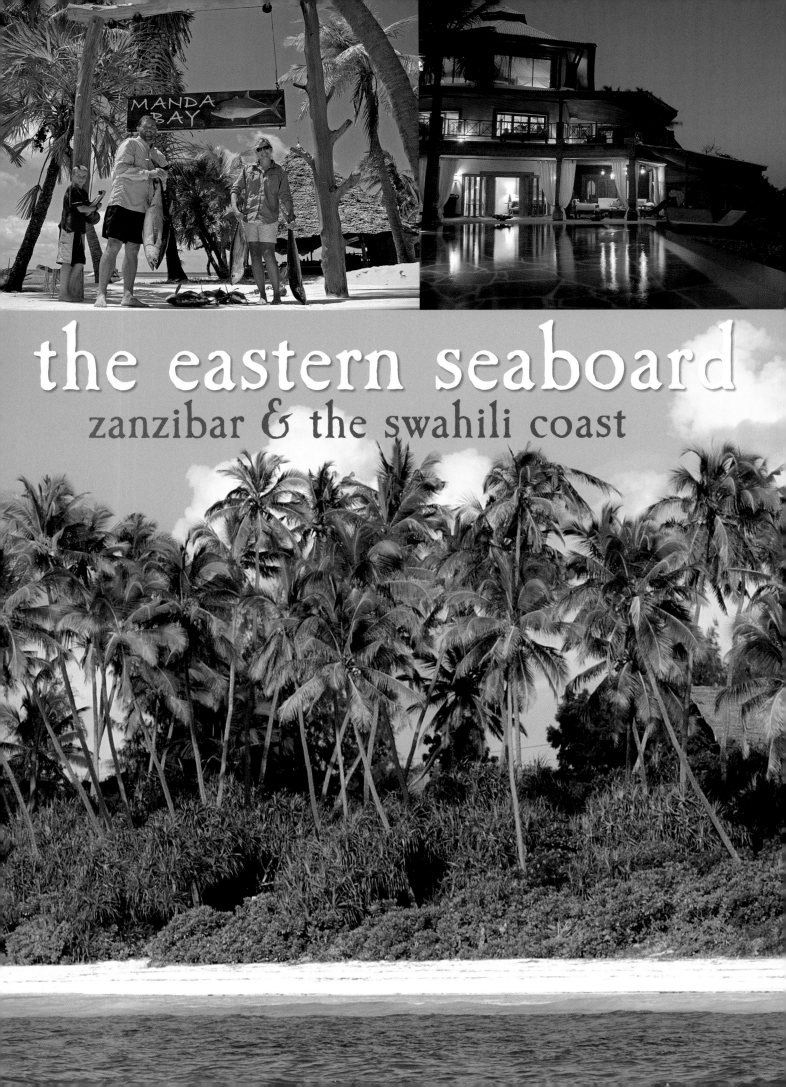

the eastern seaboard
zanzibar & the swahili coast

The spice-laden air and mystique of Zanzibar are an ideal contrast to the dust, drama and wildlife of Tanzania's safari circuit. Here other opportunities beckon: the culture and history of Stone Town, diving in crystal-clear waters, or simply lazing on a palm-fringed beach. The Arab–Swahili influence extends northwards along the Kenyan coast, embracing Mombasa, Malindi and the magical Lamu Archipelago, with its World Heritage Site of Lamu Town and laid-back Manda Island.

Near Matemwe Bungalows, north-eastern Zanzibar

alfajiri villas
diani beach, south of mombasa

Privacy is guaranteed at this luxurious hideaway

in an idyllic setting overlooking the Indian Ocean.

After hours in a Jeep bumping and lurching over dusty roads through the hinterlands in search of game, my arrival on Kenya's southern coast was greeted with a broad Swahili smile, icy fresh lime juice and an equally cold spice-scented cloth. Then my weary eyes alighted on waving coconut palms, coconut-leaf-roofed villas and a shady veranda with huge, hand-carved furniture, and my tiredness vanished completely. I had arrived at Alfajiri, an exclusive retreat perched on coral cliffs above Diani Beach. This is Kenya's Swahili coast, where the first Arab trader came to sell his goods and stayed to settle some 1 500 years ago.

Walking through impressive doors, hand-carved on Lamu Island, and down a path under flowering flamboyants, I was immediately soothed by Alfajiri's sense of privacy. This large property, owned and designed by Italians Fabrizio and Marika Molinaro, consists of three separate villas, each with stunning views of the Indian Ocean. Décor is a marriage of casual-chic Mediterranean-style comfort and exotic Swahili design details. One is spoilt for choice: the Beach Villa has two Balinese-style bedrooms, both with *en-suite* bathrooms; the Garden Villa sleeps eight guests in individually themed bedrooms, each furnished with items from countries around the world; and Cliff Villa, the favourite of actors desirous of total privacy, hunkers down on the ancient coral bluff and has its own horizon pool, which appears to merge with the Indian Ocean. Two storeys high, the master bedroom at Cliff Villa offers panoramic ocean views through plate-glass windows. The villa sleeps eight.

Décor is a marriage of *casual-chic* Mediterranean-style comfort and *exotic* Swahili design details

PREVIOUS SPREAD Alfajiri's management promises a holiday second to none. Here the sitting room, romantically lit, invites guests to relax.

THIS SPREAD Cliff Villa guarantees complete privacy.

Guests at Cliff Villa are served by a personal butler.

Diani Beach is a popular launch site for big-game fishermen.

Kenyans are known for their friendliness and easy-going temperament.

Cliff Villa's double-volume bedroom has a marquee-style ceiling and striking views.

Around the villas, lush gardens, filled with palms from the villa's own nursery, reverberate with the calls of birds and the chattering of colobus monkeys and impish vervets, which scamper across the rooftops.

The service at Alfajiri (which means 'sunrise') is effortless, efficient and discreet. Twenty staff, including nannies and butlers, are poised to cater to your every need. The Mediterranean cuisine too, could not be faulted. We fell upon wholesome fruit, seafood, vegetables, garden salads and pasta. If we so desired, reflexology and massage were offered to soothe any stubborn remaining aches and pains.

Activities are numerous. I strolled along the soft white sandy beaches (Diani Beach stretches eight kilometres to the north and eight kilometres to the south). You can also head out to sea on a jetski in search of dolphins and whale sharks, go snorkelling, play golf on a neighbouring course or chill out with a soothing massage while listening to the ocean. Nearby Pemba Channel also offers some of the best deep-sea fishing and diving in the world, something definitely not to be missed. Game drives and walking safaris can be organised to Tsavo East National Park.

A treasure worth exploring from Alfajiri is the Kisiti-Mpungati Marine National Park, which lies about eight kilometres offshore. You can only get there by boat, and it's worth every minute. Here coral gardens teeming with some 250 fish species extend for 28 square kilometres. Shallow waters and generally good visibility make this a snorkeller's dream. Dolphin-sighting trips aboard dhows can also be arranged.

Entrance to Garden Villa is via a shaggy-thatched passage.

The Ivory Room at Garden Villa.

Cliff Villa lies above a sandy beach.

Swimming pools tempt guests after a day on the beach.

Colobus monkeys are mainly arboreal in habit.

lush gardens reverberate with the *calls of birds* and the *chattering* of colobus monkeys and impish vervets

details

When to go
Alfajiri is open all year.

How to get there
Alfajiri is a one-hour drive from Mombasa Airport. Private charters and a daily service use Ukunda Airstrip, which is five minutes by road from the lodge. There is a daily air service to and from the Masai Mara National Reserve.

Who to contact
Tel. (+254-40) 320 2630, e-mail *molinaro@africaonline.co.ke* or go to *www.alfajirivillas.com*

manda bay lodge
manda island

Turquoise waters, rustling palms, tranquil cottages, underwater coral gardens and endless sun have long lured visitors to this remote corner of the Lamu archipelago.

The islands of the Lamu Archipelago, off the northern coast of Kenya, were first settled by Arab merchants between the ninth and 12th centuries, although they were mentioned by the first-century astronomer and geographer Ptolemy in his book *Ptolemy's Geography*. Four islands make up the archipelago, with Lamu Island being the principal of the group. Its chief town, Lamu Town, is one of the oldest Swahili towns in existence and is now a World Heritage Site.

Across a narrow channel to the north-east of Lamu is Manda Island, once a centre of ivory, slave and rhino-horn trading. Having arrived on Manda Island on a scheduled flight from Nairobi, I made my way to the dock, where the water taxis ferrying passengers across to Lamu were full and busy, a testament to the increasing popularity of the island. I boarded a small motorboat and headed in the opposite direction, taking a 30-minute winding journey through mangroves to the island's northern tip.

There, on a secluded peninsula far from the hurly-burly of the island's busy south, lies the small boutique resort of Manda Bay. Twelve spacious thatched cottages, sheltered by palms and tamarind trees, line the beach overlooking the Indian Ocean. Each is fronted by a huge veranda, and the interiors are simply but comfortably furnished with king-sized beds, white linen, ceiling fans that gently ruffle the air, and *en-suite* bathrooms with showers and fluffy towels. The owners Andy and Caragh Roberts and Fuzz and Bimbi Dyer live on the island, and they have taken every care to ensure that

guests' needs are met and a convivial atmosphere prevails.

There is so much to do here, with most of the activities based on the ocean. During my stay, fellow guests hired the resort's boat, *Utamaduni*, one of the largest single-mast dhows on the East African coast. Built by the master boat-builders of Lamu, this six-sleeper craft and its crew can be used for daily outings or overnight trips through the archipelago, or simply for sundowners. They returned later in the day, flushed and happy from a day in the sun and the below-sea wonders investigated through their goggles.

I could have gone snorkelling to explore the coral gardens, or chosen waterskiing, windsurfing or sailing. The fishing is spectacular, with an abundance of species such as blue, striped and black marlin and sailfish, and many other game fish that migrate through these waters. One can explore the island on foot, or take a trip to Siyu Fort, a wonderfully preserved Arab stronghold at the end of the Siyu Channel. Birdwatching and cultural visits are other options. Instead, I elected to rest on the beach, fortified with long cool drinks, brought by a laid-back but attentive waiter.

Lunch was a gourmet affair of fresh seafood, Swahili spices and tropical fruit. A consignment of giant mangrove crabs had just been delivered by a local fisherman, and I tucked into the best crab feast I'd ever had. That evening, dinner was served on the beach, lit warmly by a large fire and the soft glow of the setting sun.

PREVIOUS SPREAD To sail, swim, snorkel or snooze in the sun... the choice of leisure activities at Manda Bay is intoxicating.

THIS SPREAD There are rich pickings for game fishermen in the Indian Ocean waters.

The cuisine at Manda Bay is glorious, with a fruit and seafood bias.

The lodge's romantic bedrooms blend rustic furniture and plush comfort.

From the verandas, guests never tire of the ever-changing patterns of light on water.

There's plenty for the younger, more boisterous members of the family to do.

details

When to go
Manda Bay is closed for the rainy season, from mid-May to mid-July.

How to get there
There is a daily scheduled flight from Nairobi to Lamu.

Who to contact
E-mail *bookings@mandabay.com* or go to *www.mandabay.com*

matemwe
bungalows
zanzibar

An extraordinary marine life will enchant visitors to this laid-back

lodge on the north-eastern tip of Zanzibar's main island, Unguja.

I love islands. There is the gentle breeze that blows off the sea, the feel of salt on your skin and the wonderful white beaches and blue seas. It's also blissfully uncomplicated to go on holiday with little more than a few T-shirts, a bathing costume, sarong and a pair of shorts. So it was at Matemwe Bungalows – a romantic tropical destination on the remote north-eastern shores of Unguja, the biggest island in Tanzania's Zanzibar archipelago.

Matemwe is one of the smallest lodges on the island with just 15 bungalows, including three new romantic honeymoon suites. All offer spectacular views of the Indian Ocean. Each morning I threw open the large wooden doors to my private veranda and sipped my coffee as the sun rose over the sea and two or three lateen-rigged *ngalawas* from the local village headed across the turquoise waters to their fishing grounds. To the south a white beach, fringed by a long line of swaying palm trees, stretched for 800 metres, beckoning me to explore. The gentle walk was just long enough to work up an appetite for breakfast.

Guests at the lodge include newlyweds enjoying a blissful honeymoon, or holidaymakers simply wanting nothing more than to relax with a book by the swimming pool (there are two pools: one gives a feeling of swimming in the sea, while the other is more sheltered from the elements) or to wander along the beach. On the shore, an open-air bar was decorated with a dhow and the skeletal remains of a sperm whale which had washed up on the sand. Here, waiters in white tunics lined up to prepare all manner of cocktails, or a cup of tea. Afterwards, I strolled back to the lodge to use their Internet facility to catch up with news from home and send images back to show what a great time I was having.

The garden pulsated with fragrant frangipani, bougainvilleas, palms and a host of other exotic plants, but I was most taken by the concrete sculptures: giant tortoises, an octopus draped over the swimming pool and a larger-than-life ghost crab, all constructed by local artists Salvador Casmiro and Burton Benedict. During my stay they were creating an outdoor chess set, with the black pieces fashioned from ebony and each taking more than two weeks to complete.

Local workmanship is also reflected in the bungalows, with their thatched roofs, and furniture and wide, heavy doors made from indigenous timber. When I checked in, my room was filled with the heady scent of hundreds of flowers, which had been arranged on the bed and in the bathroom.

In the evenings, barbecues were offered in the open-sided dining area overlooking the ocean. On other occasions there was always a wide variety of dishes to choose from, with fish being the culinary highlight. As I'd watched the local fishermen carrying their daily catch of yellowtail, red snapper, steenbras, crayfish, octopus and the occasional marlin up the beach to the lodge, there was no doubt as to the freshness of their harvest.

The sea is obviously one of the main attractions here, and the swimming is great. At low tide, the water recedes to expose a rocky reef, which stretches for several hundred metres in front of the lodge, marooning all craft. Many visitors take advantage of this time to relax on the hammocks on their verandas, but it also offers the perfect opportunity to

Each morning I threw open the large wooden doors to my private veranda and sipped my coffee as the *sun rose over the sea*

PREVIOUS SPREAD Like low-flying kites, lateen-rigged dhows scud past Matemwe Bungalows.

THIS SPREAD Matemwe is in a startlingly beautiful location, with tropical vegetation and aquamarine water.

Fishermen prepare for a day at sea.

The bungalows offer sheltered seclusion from other visitors.

Harvest from the sea features prominently on the menu.

walk along the beach, have a massage, or to visit nearby Stone Town or other island attractions. The lodge has fostered a close relationship with the neighbouring fishing village of Kigomani. Here visitors are encouraged to explore Zanzibar culture and village life. I saw dhows and *ngalawas* pulled up on the shore, small houses made of coral, men working on boats and nets, and women drying seaweed on racks. The lodge cooperates with the community by purchasing their fish catch, providing employment and making a donation to the village school each year.

High tide brings a plethora of marine activities. Sea-kayaking, deep-sea fishing and scuba diving are popular. I opted for snorkelling and was entranced by the richness of the underwater life, from soft and hard corals, sponges and sea anemones to shoals of fish in every hue imaginable. Marine-life enthusiasts could also choose to take a 30-minute boat ride to Mnemba Atoll, a five-kilometre-long and three-kilometre-wide reef that forms part of a marine park. Here snorkelling will reveal a fairyland of vivid corals and tropical fishes, including angelfish, fusiliers, wrasses and kingfishes.

Snorkelling is a popular pastime.

Leaning palms and tropical undergrowth edge the beach.

Dinner by the light of a hundred lanterns.

Scattered blossoms and artfully arranged towels await you in your bungalow.

snorkelling will reveal a *fairyland of vivid corals* and tropical fishes, including angelfish, fusiliers...

details

When to go
The lodge is open all year except during the rainy season in April and May. For the rest of the year expect warm conditions and tropical bliss. June is usually clear, but can be quite windy.

How to get there
There are daily flights to Zanzibar International Airport and it's a further 90-minute drive to Matemwe.

Who to contact
Tel. (+255-27) 250 4118, e-mail *info@asilialodges.com* or go to *www.asilialodges.com*

the central highlands
tsavo, laikipia & northern kenya

Mount Shompole, Kenya

Kenya's uplands are particularly rich in wildlife. From Tsavo East National Park westwards, past the capital of Nairobi and across the Laikipia Plateau, there is a plethora of game sanctuaries. At the country's heart is Mount Kenya, Africa's second-highest mountain. The northern reaches are remote, often scorchingly hot and sparsely populated by nomadic pastoralists. Here, helicopter flights over the volcanic plains and the swamps and riverine forests formed by the Ewaso N'giro River offer excellent opportunities to see the game.

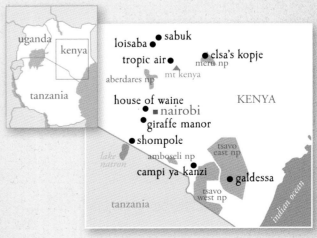

uganda
kenya
tanzania

loisaba ● ● sabuk
tropic air ● ● elsa's kopje
aberdares np meru np
mt kenya
house of waine KENYA
● ■ nairobi
● giraffe manor
● shompole
lake natron
amboseli np
tsavo east np
campi ya kanzi ● galdessa
tanzania tsavo west np
indian ocean

campi ya kanzi

chyulu hills

Campi ya Kanzi is Kiswahili for 'Camp of the Hidden Treasure',

and this luxury safari getaway is, indeed, a real gem.

Food is grown in an *organic garden*, watered with recycled water — small wonder that this is the *most awarded eco-lodge* in Africa

PREVIOUS SPREAD If you like, your Campi ya Kanzi safari walk can include breakfast in the bush.

THIS SPREAD Each tent has a wide veranda from which to view your private patch of Africa.

Evenings are a convivial blend of good company, fine wines and fireside tales.

Coke's hartebeest inhabit the plains and lightly wooded areas of central Tanzania to central Kenya.

Preparing for dinner.

Walking on the Chyulu Hills.

Campi ya Kanzi shimmered like a vivid emerald in a sea of sand. All around, evidence could be seen of the drought that held Kenya in its grip: to the south-west, Amboseli was a dust bowl; to the south and east, not a blade of grass brightened the landscape of Tsavo. Yet here the Chyulu Hills were covered in a mantle of green. It suddenly became evident why Ernest Hemingway, when writing his book about the Chyulus, called it 'Green Hills of Africa'.

These hills are infants in geological terms – they were formed by volcanic action just 500 years ago. Their rounded domes are punctuated by volcanic vents and dark lava flows. Water percolates through them, forming deep and fast-flowing subterranean rivers that feed the hills and, to the south, the Mzima Springs in Tsavo West National Park.

Campi ya Kanzi is set in the foothills of the Chyulus on Kuku Group Ranch, a joint venture owned by the local Maasai community and Italians Luca and Antonella Belpietro, who share a passion for Africa. 'When I came here for the first time,' said Antonella, 'I saw a paradise on earth and knew I had to live here.' The ranch sprawls across 1 150 square kilometres, on land that climbs from 1 000 to 2 300 metres above sea level, encompassing a biodiversity of montane forest, grasslands, verdant river woodlands, scrubby bush, savanna, lakes and inselbergs.

I was met with a warm welcome and a traditional song by Maasai women. The Belpietros are kind and generous hosts, whose thoughtful touches, including the warm towels and cold drinks in my room, made me feel thoroughly at home. Mine was one of seven luxury thatched, tented cottages built on stilted platforms far enough apart to ensure complete privacy. Electricity is supplied by solar panels, hot water by solar boilers. Food is grown in an organic garden, watered with recycled water – small wonder that this is the most awarded eco-lodge in Africa.

The central meeting place is Tembo House, constructed of local lava rocks and roofed with grass. Here we took our meals (fine Italian cuisine prepared by trained local chefs), relaxed or researched our day's sightings in the library, or sat on the veranda, drinks in hand, and gazed upon the sweeping vista. The décor throughout is a comfortable, stylish blend of Italian chic and Maasai ornamentation. My bedroom had beds made from local wood and bedlinen imported from Italy.

Safaris are arranged to suit your needs. Maasai guides will escort you on game walks across the savanna plains or up into the cloud forests of the Chyulu Hills. Alternatively, take a mobile safari and sleep in a fly tent on the slopes of Mount Kilimanjaro. For the less athletic, game drives are offered, ending with sundowners on top of huge granite inselbergs with majestic views.

Wildlife is abundant. There are about 63 mammal species here, with the big five joined by less common lesser kudu, gerenuk, fringe-eared oryx, wild dog and many others. Bird-lovers will enjoy ticking the 400 bird species. The camp has its own aircraft, and offers early morning flights over Mount Kilimanjaro.

At the heart of Campi ya Kanzi is a concern for the environment, wildlife and the Maasai culture. For each guest accommodated at the camp, US$40 of the daily conservation fee is set aside for the community and is used to reimburse loss of livestock by predation, to help students with their education and to provide the community with basic medicines.

details

When to go
There's something to see at Campi ya Kanzi all year.

How to get there
Book a trip through your local travel agent, who will arrange a flight to Nairobi, from where it's a one-hour flight in the camp's aircraft, or a six-hour trip in a 4x4. Flights can also be arranged from Mombasa and Malindi.

Who to contact
E-mail *lucasaf@africaonline.co.ke* or go to *www.maasai.com*

elsa's kopje
meru national park

Meru National Park has recovered from hard times to re-establish itself as one of Kenya's prime game-viewing areas. Sited in its western savanna plains, Elsa's Kopje offers luxurious living and plentiful wildlife.

My private veranda proved *irresistible*, and I spent a lazy hour watching the plains game

When I first visited Meru National Park 12 years ago it was barely running: the animals were very shy and the pressures of poaching had made the elephants aggressive. Now I was due to return, and I held slim hope for what my first game drive would reveal. So I was hugely surprised to come across a large breeding herd of elephants, who allowed us to approach without any aggression. I was also astonished to drive through some of the biggest herds of buffalo I've ever seen without being covered in a cloud of dust drummed up by their retreating hooves. We came across a pride of lions who had killed a buffalo the evening before, as well as herds of reticulated giraffe and, a real treat, the shy lesser kudu.

Meru National Park forms part of an ecosystem that includes Kora, Rahole and Bisanadi reserves, making it a huge conservation area. The park itself covers 181 300 hectares, and has some of the wildest country in Kenya. To the north are the foothills of the Nyambeni Hills, while the Tana River marks the eastern border. In the west, wooded grasslands form a hilly upland drained by 15 permanent streams. Baobab trees dot the savanna, and dense ribbons of doum and raphia palms grow along the valleys.

Meru, established in 1968, is famous for its association with the film *Born Free*, about George and Joy Adamson and their work with the orphaned lioness, Elsa. In its prime, the park received thousands of visitors a year but, in the 1970s and 1980s, rampant poaching was rife. Rhino and elephant numbers were decimated, and some Belgian tourists were killed, as was George Adamson, who was murdered in Kora by poachers. As a final blow, the bushmeat trade of the 1990s reduced the park to a dire state. Then, with the appointment of head warden Mark Jenkins, security and infrastructure was improved. In addition, the Kenya Wildlife Service undertook translocation programmes to restore game levels. Just two success stories have been the re-introduction of black and white rhinos, which are flourishing in their protected sanctuary within the park, and the birth of a white rhino in 2003.

It's here that I discovered Kenya's best-kept secret – Elsa's Kopje, a lodge built on top of Mughwango Hill, the site of George Adamson's first camp, called Elsa's Camp. It is easy to see why he chose this site, elevated above the plains. From the top, you can see forever. Yet the lodge blends so well with the rocky crags and bush that it is almost invisible from below. Each of the nine individually designed cottages offers complete privacy. All are different: some have great boulders as walls, others have baths with water flowing over rocks. Across a suspension bridge, two cottages have been set apart for couples and honeymooners.

My thatched, double-storeyed chalet had two trees growing through it, indicating the care for environment taken in its design. I had a large bed, swathed in netting, and an *en-suite* bathroom built against a natural boulder wall. My private veranda, with its comfortable cushioned chairs, proved irresistible, and I spent a lazy hour watching the plains game – an elephant family, giraffes and numerous antelope species – moving across the grasslands. Later we took sundowners at the hippo pools, with doum palms silhouetted against the dimming sky, before returning to camp for dinner, an inspired combination of traditional north Italian fare and the freshest local ingredients. Following the paved, lamp-lit path back to my cottage, I felt embraced by the comfort of the surroundings and the velvety African night.

PREVIOUS SPREAD Smiling waiters deliver refreshments at your request.

With its hilltop location and wide verandas, Elsa's Kopje is the perfect site from which to observe the plains.

THIS SPREAD A spa experience on the wild side.

The rhino population at Meru National Park is growing, with a white rhino born in 2003.

A romantic dinner by the pool.

Elsa's Kopje lodge and pool meld with their surroundings.

Construction has incorporated nature, with some rooms built around existing trees.

details

When to go
Elsa's Kopje is open all year.

How to get there
There's a daily one-hour scheduled flight from Jomo Kenyatta International Airport operated by Air Kenya and Safari Link. Another daily flight operated by Tropic Air travels from Nanyuki to Meru (40 minutes). By road, it's a six-hour trip from Nairobi.

Who to contact
For information or reservations, contact Cheli & Peacock, tel. (+254-20) 60 4053, e-mail *safaris@chelipeacock.co.ke* or go to *www.chelipeacock.com*

galdessa camp
tsavo east national park

With two camps squatting beneath doum palms on the banks of the Galana River, Galdessa offers the pinnacle of stylish safaris – the excitement of wild Africa combined with eco-friendly creature comforts.

PREVIOUS SPREAD Sundowners, an attentive butler and a gently flowing river induce a peaceful reverie.

THIS SPREAD Elephants have crossed the Galana River at this spot for centuries.

Partially secluded by trees, Galdessa Camp lies on the southern bank of the Galana River.

The lodge and bandas have been thatched with the leaves of makuti palms.

Scanning the plains from Mudanda Rock, a 1.6-kilometre-long outcrop of stratified rock.

A bedroom at Galdessa.

Hidden in a clump of doum palms, I stand silently as family groups of elephants approach the river. They come from all directions, first drinking and then splashing across to the other side. It's an awe-inspiring sight, and heartening to see these magnificent beasts so healthy and contented. This hasn't always been the case.

I'm in the Tsavo National Park, a 2.1-million-hectare swathe of untamed grassland in southern Kenya bisected by the Mombasa Highway into Tsavo East and Tsavo West. In the 1960s, Tsavo supported an elephant population of around 70 000. By 1972 this number had been slashed by drought and starvation; by the late 1980s, poaching had reduced the count even further – just 5 000 remained. Now, thanks to careful husbandry by the Kenya Wildlife Service (KWS), the population is growing.

My companions are an armed KWS ranger and an old poacher from the legendary elephant-hunting Waliangulu ('People of the Long Bow') tribe, whose pursuit of wildlife has been curtailed through legislation. Following in the footsteps of the poacher, we've been exploring the banks of the Galana River, and he's brought us to this ancient elephant crossing and drinking spot. Quietly he explains to us how, many years ago, he and his fellow poachers would wait in ambush at this very place for the elephants, which have been coming down from the plateau along the same path for hundreds of years. Now, instead of leading a hunting party, he uses his knowledge to show these special places to visitors.

Galdessa Camp is situated on the south bank of the Galana River in Tsavo East, just one kilometre upstream from this elephant-watching spot. South-west of the camp is the 290-kilometre-long Yatta Plateau, the world's longest and oldest fossilised lava flow. Further downstream are Lugard's Falls, actually a series of rapids named after the first British governor in East Africa.

This is a luxury camp *par excellence*. It is divided into two lodges, each with its own private lounge and bar overlooking the Galana River. The main lodge consists of 11 spacious bandas; the smaller, private camp has just three. Each tented banda is built on stilts, with a makuti-thatched roof to ensure cool and shade, an *en-suite* bathroom and a private wooden veranda on which to enjoy sundowners. Two bandas are designed especially

Hidden in a clump
of doum palms, I
stand silently as family
groups of elephants
approach the river

for honeymooners, with separate verandas on stilts enabling them to sleep safely under the stars while listening to the night-time shuffling of elephants and hippos. Solar power provides lighting and hot water, with bucket showers filled at your request by your personal butler.

The beauty of Galdessa is its natural ambience and décor. The bandas, with their sweeping roofs, merge into the surroundings. The wooden decks and furniture are made of local timber; bones, feathers and quills are woven into the interior design. But don't be fooled by the simplicity – the service and attention to detail are sophisticated and luxurious. Meals at Galdessa are wholesome, tasty and exquisitely presented. And if you are vegetarian or have other dietary constraints, your needs will be met with a smile.

The riverside location of the lodges ensures constant sightings of wild-life along its banks, including a rich and varied birdlife. You can explore the Galana and other routes along its seasonal tributaries in open 4x4 vehicles. As they often have permanent pools, these rivers are the favour-ite haunt of lions, leopards, elephants, buffaloes and rhinos. Within the immediate area of the camps, there are more than 50 black rhinos, testa-ment to the owners' successful rhino conservation policy. As one guest said, 'At Galdessa, the animals come to you'.

You can also take a guided walking safari along the river, while longer game drives can be arranged to Tsavo East's farther reaches. On these day outings, the ever-attentive staff will probably surprise you with a three-course picnic lunch, complete with iced drinks. And it's highly likely that a shout from your guide drawing your attention to 'a leopard with a kill' will instead reveal upon closer inspection a beautiful break-fast spread in a dry riverbed under the rustling doum palms!

Little Galdessa lodge has just three bandas.

Guests can sleep beneath the stars on Little Galdessa's stilted verandas.

The ideal spot for a honeymoon ... or just to get away from it all.

Pre-dinner drinks can be taken in the camp's lounge.

The European roller is widespread throughout the savannas of East Africa.

The riverside location of the lodge ensures *constant sightings* of wildlife, including a *rich and varied* birdlife

details

When to go
Galdessa Camp is closed in May.

How to get there
The camp is a one-hour flight from Nairobi. By road, it is a three-and-a-half-hour drive from Mombasa, and four-and-a-half hours from Nairobi.

Who to contact
Exclusive Classic Properties on tel. (+254-20) 712 3156/712 0943, e-mail *galdessa@swiftkenya.com* or go to *www.galdessa.com*

giraffe manor

near nairobi

Rothschild's giraffes roam freely in the grounds of this elegant manor house on the outskirts of the Kenyan capital.

Maasai legend has it that the Ngong Hills, which are shaped like the knuckles of a clenched fist, were formed when a giant tripped over Mount Kilimanjaro 250 kilometres to the south, clawing at the earth as he fell. As the sun sets behind these gnarled hills, its rays illuminate the Nairobi suburb of Karen. There, set in a vast forest, you will see a gabled 1930s manor house in the Scottish hunting lodge style. Its tranquillity is a far cry from the thrum of the capital city. Like all large cities, central Nairobi is abuzz with humanity. Yet just 20 minutes by road will bring you to this unique manor house, with its cavorting warthogs and curious giraffes.

The property was purchased in 1974 by Jock and Betty Leslie-Melville. When Jock died, Betty opened her home to visitors. Now her son Rick Anderson and his wife Bryony own Giraffe Manor, and they welcome guests with a warmth that typifies this couple's passion for their country and its wildlife.

The rooms are styled for all manner of visitors. Honeymooners enjoy the master bedroom with its art-deco bathroom and views of the Ngong Hills. Families with children feel most comfortable in the Giraffe Room or in the Karen Blixen annexe, which has its own fireplace and sitting area and is decorated with Blixen's original furniture and wildlife paintings executed by her talented cook, Kamante.

Dining is in an elegantly wood-panelled room with many-candled candelabras. Again, children are well catered for, with shepherd's pie or pasta suppers served early on request. For adults, dinner is always a surprise, as the manor is popular among the world's glitterati, and you never know who your dining companions will be. After-dinner cognac and port can be savoured in the cosy drawing room.

giraffes will *pop their heads* through the windows of the breakfast room to see what's on the menu

PREVIOUS SPREAD Long-necked guests investigate what's for tea.

THIS SPREAD The manor's namesakes are evident even in the décor.

Rothschild's giraffes, the tallest of the giraffes, were once widespread on the Soy Plain.

The giraffes at the manor are completely tame.

Each bedroom is decorated with its own style.

The sitting room.

But it's the giraffes who are the real stars here. Ten rare, endangered Rothschild's giraffes roam the estate freely, and you're quite likely to be greeted in the morning by the appearance through your bedroom window of a long-necked lovely sporting luxuriant lashes and an elongated tongue. Later, the giraffes will pop their heads through the windows of the breakfast room to greet guests and see what's on the menu. The first of the herd was Daisy, who was saved from poachers on Kenya's Soy Plain in the 1970s and brought to Nairobi in a VW Kombi. Her tale is told in the book *Raising Daisy Rothschild* and in the TV movie *The Last Giraffe*.

Attached to Giraffe Manor is the Giraffe Centre, run by the African Foundation for Endangered Wildlife, which was founded in 1978 by the Leslie-Melvilles. This organisation is responsible for the increase in the number of Rothschild's giraffes in Kenya from 130 to over 300. Another project is the first educational nature sanctuary in independent Africa, and in 2005 over 55 000 schoolchildren visited the centre free of charge to learn about their wildlife heritage. Here they see and feed the giraffes and warthogs, and walk through the Jock Leslie-Melville Sanctuary with an educational officer who teaches them about environmental protection matters. Thus the animals are saved and a future is secured for the people who rely on tourism for income and employment.

details

When to go
Giraffe Manor is closed from 15 April to 15 May and from 24 to 26 December.

How to get there
The manor is 12 kilometres west of central Nairobi, and 45 minutes by road from Nairobi International Airport.

Who to contact
Tel. (+254-20) 89 1078, fax (+254-20) 89 0949, e-mail *giraffe@giraffemanor.com* or go to *www.giraffemanor.com*

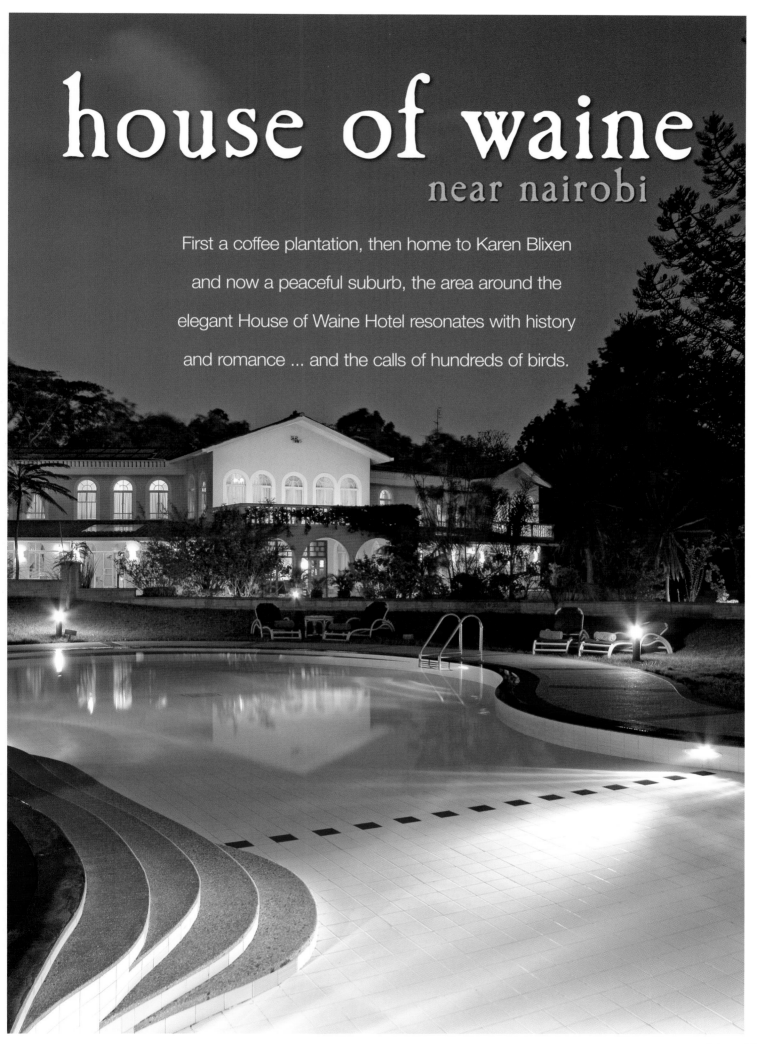

house of waine

near nairobi

First a coffee plantation, then home to Karen Blixen and now a peaceful suburb, the area around the elegant House of Waine Hotel resonates with history and romance ... and the calls of hundreds of birds.

PREVIOUS SPREAD Teatime at House of Waine is a lavish ritual.

The hotel is entirely African controlled and managed.

THIS SPREAD Intimate dinners can be taken in the pavilion.

The Tembo guest room.

Fine cuisine is a fitting end to a day of sightseeing.

The entrance arbour and veranda.

No expense has been spared – even the
swimming pool is heated.

Large gardens with
indigenous olive
and croton trees and
*voluptuous hibiscus
bushes* surround the
main house

In 1911, a 2 000-hectare parcel of land at the foot of the Ngong Hills was purchased by the Swedo-African Coffee Company to develop as a plantation. Two years later the business was acquired by Danish Baron Bror von Blixen-Finecke for his wife, Karen. Her attempts to grow coffee were unsuccessful, but she made her home on the estate from 1917 to 1931, and her experiences during this period are famously portrayed in the film of her life, *Out of Africa*. When Blixen returned to Denmark in 1931, the estate was broken up for development and it is here, in the serene, wooded suburb of Karen, just 30 minutes from the pulsating hub of Nairobi, that the tranquil boutique hotel, House of Waine, is found. Built in the 1970s as a private residence, the present owners (whose first-name initials spell the name 'Waine') have created an exclusive family-run hotel that is wholly African controlled and managed.

Large gardens with indigenous olive and croton trees and voluptuous hibiscus bushes surround the main house. Inside are 11 individually decorated luxurious guest suites, from the deep-red, Maasai-inspired Manyatta room to the blue-green, island-style Pwani room. All have marble *en-suite* bathrooms. After a day's sightseeing, an enormous heated swimming pool invites you to take a plunge.

Breakfast and lunch are served indoors, on the sunny terrace or in the garden, where one morning I was lucky enough to see a Hartlaub's turaco, an African green-pigeon and a Kikuyu white-eye all in single tree. If twitching is in your blood, then this is the place for you – the Karen area has a bird count of more than 265 species.

During the British occupation of Kenya, '*Tafadhali leta chai na kahawa*' would have been a phrase heard in dining and sitting rooms throughout the country. It means 'Please bring tea and coffee'. There's no need to ask at the House of Waine. Every afternoon, the delicious aroma of freshly brewed Kenyan coffee and tea tempted me onto the terrace, where a spread of pastries and cookies kept me munching until long shadows started to form at the poolside.

This is the perfect place to stay when you're visiting Nairobi; many of the city's major attractions are an easy five-minutes' drive away. Just around the corner is the Karen Blixen National Museum, in the house in which she lived, set in a park-like garden of Norfolk pines, palms, cypresses and candelabra euphorbia trees.

Also nearby is the Giraffe Centre, a breeding ranch for rare Rothschild's giraffes, and the Daphne Sheldrick Animal Orphanage. Nairobi National Park is just 10-minutes' drive to the east, and offers the superb opportunity to see rare black rhino, lions, cheetahs and all of East Africa's plains game, plus some of the best birding in Kenya.

details

When to go
House of Waine is open all year.

How to get there
Both Nairobi city centre and Jomo Kenyatta International Airport are 30 minutes away by road.

Who to contact
Tel. (+254-20) 89 1820/89 1553, e-mail *mail@houseofwaine.co.ke* or go to *www.houseofwaine.com*

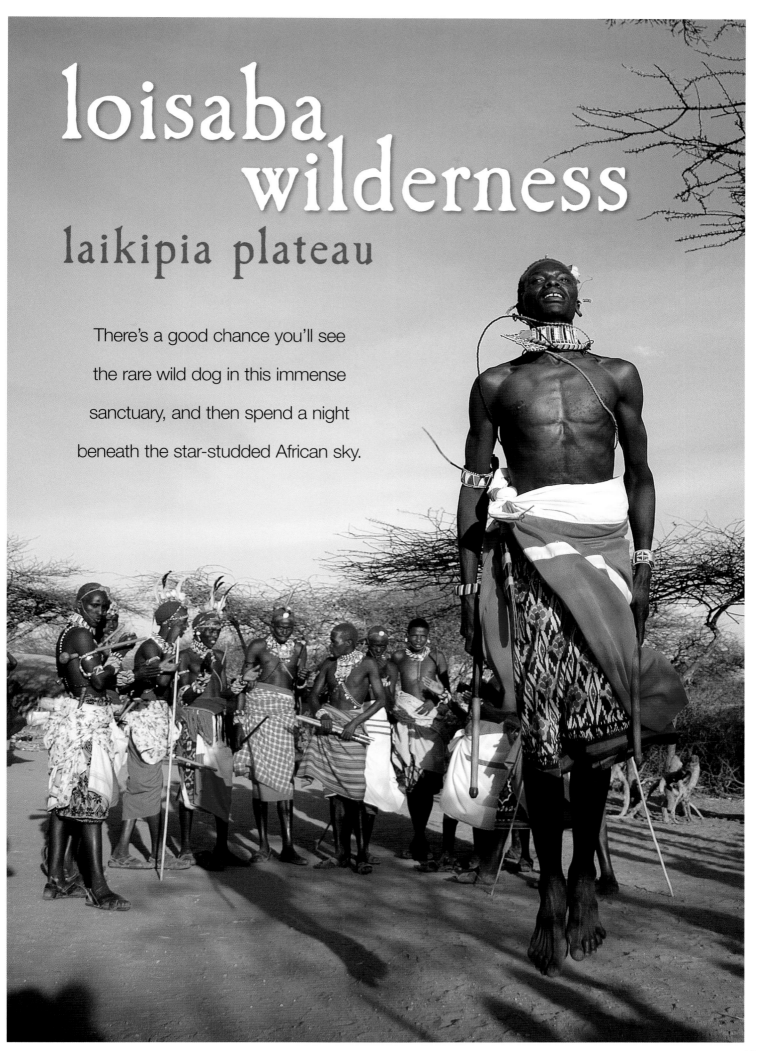

loisaba
wilderness
laikipia plateau

There's a good chance you'll see the rare wild dog in this immense sanctuary, and then spend a night beneath the star-studded African sky.

The Laikipia Plateau, west of Mount Kenya, is home to more endangered animals than anywhere else in the country. It is the last bastion of the Lelwel hartebeest, the rangeland of thousands of elephants, and its rolling hills hold more than half the country's rhino population. Laikipia also has one of the few growing populations of wild dogs, one of the world's most endangered canids. On the northern edge of this remarkable area is Loisaba Wilderness, a 25 000-hectare, privately managed wildlife conservancy.

I stayed at the stone, cedar and palm-thatched Loisaba Lodge, constructed high on the edge of a 300-metre-plateau looking south towards Mount Kenya. My room had large French windows, each opening on to a private deck cantilevered dizzyingly off the escarpment. The views defy description, and I was mesmerised by the continuous stream of animals coming and going from a waterhole below. The lodge has a swimming pool, tennis court and croquet lawn.

There are other alternatives for accommodation – Loisaba House and Loisaba Cottage each cater for four people. In addition, two singularly unusual places to stay at Loisaba are Star Beds (loisaba is a Samburu word meaning 'seven stars'), camps that have been created in a joint venture with the Laikipia Maasai people. Kiboko Star Beds squats among rocks in an eastern valley overlooking the Kiboko waterholes, while its Koija equivalent perches high on the banks of the Ewaso N'giro River, on community-owned land, and is reached by footbridge from the opposite bank. Each room is dramatically designed with a pointed thatch roof, wooden platform and hand-carved furniture. Here I was

well looked after by a team of Samburu warriors in traditional dress, who would wheel out my unusual *mkokoteni* double bed onto the deck area for a night in the open. Under my thick duvet, amply shrouded with netting to repel the mosquitoes, my ceiling became the infinite dark sky, sequinned with stars.

The Loisaba wilderness area is the same size as the Ngorongoro Crater in Tanzania. On its northern boundary are the vast grassy plains of the plateau; to the south are valleys, escarpments and cliffs that frame views of distant, snow-capped Mount Kenya. In the valleys an altogether different ecosystem exists, with lush groves of acacia, fig and palm fed by the two major rivers – the Ewaso N'giro and the Ngare Narok. The wilderness is a haven for more than 250 species of birds and 50 species of mammals. I saw elephants, herds of buffalo, Grevy's zebra, reticulated giraffe and greater kudu, and the area is also rapidly gaining a reputation for big cats.

There's so much to do. I could have gone horseriding, camel-trekking, walking, taken a helicopter flip or rafting on the river. I only had time for two activities, so I chose first to take a game drive with a professionally trained Samburu guide who had studied the predators at Laikipia. It was a good call, as we encountered a pack of 17 wild dogs, the rarest of the predators to be seen in Kenya.

My second choice was the 'Quads for Classrooms'. By hiring a quad-bike, I would directly sponsor a classroom for the local community. I sped off across the savanna, comforted by the knowledge that my actions would benefit Kenya's children.

PREVIOUS SPREAD A bedroom at Loisaba Lodge.

Loisaba House and Loisaba Cottage have been created in collaboration with the Maasai people of Laikipia.

THIS SPREAD The verandas afford never-ending views across the Laikipia plains.

Hiring quad-bikes benefits Maasai schoolchildren.

Sleeping beneath the stars at Star Beds.

Samburu warriors are in discreet attendance.

The perfect chill-out area – the pool at Loisaba Lodge.

details

When to go
Loisaba Lodge, Loisaba Cottage and Star Beds are closed from mid-April to the end of May. Loisaba House is closed from 5 January to 15 June, and from 30 September to 16 December. Loisaba Star Beds is also closed in November.

How to get there
Air Kenya flies daily to Nanyuki, from where there's a charter flight to Loisaba. From Nanyuki, Tropic Air has a daily flight to the reserve. Loisaba is a six-hour drive from Nairobi.

Who to contact
For enquiries or reservations, contact Laikipia Wildlife Forum on (+254) 623 1072, e-mail *enquiries@loisaba.com* or *safaris@chelipeacock.co.ke*. Go to *www.loisaba.com* or *www.chelipeacock.com*

sabuk lodge
laikipia plateau

Game-viewing from the back of a gently undulating camel is a speciality of Sabuk, a lodge perched high above a permanent river.

The desolate, arid drylands of northern Kenya are vast, magnificent and still largely unexplored. On the western edge of this Northern Frontier District, in a plateau landscape with battlements made of scarps and fallen boulders rising out of the thorny scrub, a beautiful lodge called Sabuk is found. Perched on a cliff overlooking the Ewaso N'giro River, which flows year round through the gorge below, Sabuk provides views that are nothing short of spectacular.

Each of the lodge's five spacious stone-and-thatch cottages blends in with the harsh background. All are uniquely designed and moulded to follow the twists and turns of the ancient rocky ledges and outcrops. Each is open-fronted and equipped with gnarled wooden furniture, generous double beds protected with mosquito netting and lazy couches strewn with vivid cushions. Bathrooms are *en suite* with sumptuous deep stone baths that have the best views of all. And from the verandas, supported 45 metres above the river gorge, you can see forever. Overlooking the river is a sparkling horizon pool.

I'd heard that camel-back safaris are one of the specialities at Sabuk, and I was buoyed up by the anticipation of my first-ever camel ride. The next morning, after a delicious breakfast, I was met by a team of Laikipiak Maasai, Turkhana and Samburu guides, who have been conducting camel-back safaris for the past 20 years. Nervous of the beasts' reputation for spitting, I avoided the

Nervous of the beasts' reputation for spitting, I avoided the mouth end, but I needn't have worried

mouth end, but I needn't have worried. The camels are well trained and remarkably responsive to their Maasai handlers. I mounted and settled into an unexpectedly comfortable saddle and, having established that I was secure, we set off. The view from my elevated perch was amazing; we passed through deserted tracts of wilderness and past rock pools, and saw elephants, buffalo, reticulated giraffes, Defassa waterbuck and many dik-dik. The guides had an encyclopedic knowledge of the surrounds and pointed out signs I'd otherwise have missed, such as animal spoor and plants used for traditional medicine. There were lots of bird-calls, interspersed with periods of absolute silence.

Our destination was a small fly-camp with tents of shade-netting deep in a ravine carved by the Ewaso N'giro River. Here, after a camp-fire meal, we spent the night under the sparkling Milky Way. If camel-riding doesn't appeal, then game walks, using the camels as pack animals, are a possibility. Birdwatching was popular with some of the guests, and fishing, swimming and tubing in the river were other options.

The following day, back at camp, I spoke to Verity Williams, a Kenyan safari guide with 23 years' experience, who recently purchased Sabuk in partnership with a guest who'd returned so many times he simply couldn't leave. 'Here at Sabuk we offer a real wilderness experience,' she said. 'We concentrate mainly on walking and camel trips amongst the free-roaming game – elephants, leopards, lions, wild dogs, greater kudu, buffalo, reticulated giraffe, Grevy's and plains zebras, waterbuck, bushbuck, klipspringer, warthogs, impala and dik-dik. Some of these animals are resident, but a lot of them come and go as they please – we have no fences. The birdlife here is fantastic too, and I love the early morning 'wake-up' chorus.'

details

When to go
Sabuk Lodge is closed from the end of Easter to the end of May.

How to get there
Private charter planes fly to Loisaba airfield, and Air Kenya travels to Nanyuki, from where Tropic Air also offers scheduled flights. On arrival, guests are transported by vehicle.

Who to contact
E-mail *veritykd@africaonline.co.ke* or *sabuk@iwayafrica.com,* or go to *www. sabuklodge.com*

shompole lodge
nguruman escarpment

A jewel of a lodge on the edge of the Nguruman

Escarpment, Shompole blends cool luxury with a profusion

of game and a commitment to community development.

The world has many great mountains, lakes, deserts and oceans, but of its valleys and gorges one alone dwarfs all others in size. Indeed, the Great Rift Valley is perhaps the single most dramatic feature on earth.

A 30-minute flight south-west from Nairobi gave me breathtaking views of this incredible geological phenomenon of fissures, volcanic hills and saline lakes before we touched down in the valley below the Nguruman Escarpment in a cloud of fine volcanic dust. At 757 metres above sea level, it was hot on the ground. 'Temperatures reach 35°C for most of the year,' said Joseph, the Maasai guide, '*Hakuna matata*, don't worry. Wait until you reach the lodge'.

And so it was. There, on the edge of the escarpment, overlooking the vast plains and rift valley, I found Shompole Lodge. As I entered beneath the thatched roof, I was struck by the cool tranquillity of the interior. Water was abundantly evident throughout the complex, and 'cool pools' were a feature of each guest suite. Having been shown to my quarters, I plunged straight in and emerged rejuvenated, ready to explore the surroundings. In response to my question about the water supply, I discovered that although the annual rainfall is just 10 to 15 millimetres per year, both the escarpment and the nearby Loita Hills are a source of seasonal rivers and plentiful underground water.

Shompole consists of two lodges, the main section with six rooms, and Little Shompole, which has two private suites, a swimming pool, dining area and its own staff. The rooms throughout have been strategically designed to take advantage of the views, and on a clear day you can see as far as the

Water was abundantly evident throughout the complex, and *'cool pools' were a feature* of each guest suite

PREVIOUS SPREAD From the private decks at Little Shompole you can look across the plains to the mountain for which the lodge is named.

THIS SPREAD The rooms at Main Shompole have private pools and striking vistas.

Like those at the main lodge, the bedrooms at Little Shompole are simply but elegantly built of white quartz and fig-tree wood.

Lake Natron is the breeding ground of two million flamingos.

Joseph, like the other Maasai guides, combines guiding and lodge duties.

The free-form pool at Main Shompole.

Ngorongoro Crater in Tanzania. The style is uncluttered, with white quartz stone construction and pale fig-tree wood furniture. While the beds are cocooned in canopied canvas-and-netting tents, there are no walls to interrupt the panorama. You can even gaze at the plains while taking a shower. If you like, your meals can be delivered to your room by your personal butler. I elected to eat in the main dining and lounge area, but dinners in the bush overlooking Lake Natron or breakfast in the fig-tree forest were other tempting alternatives.

The camp is the creation of Anthony Russell, a veteran of wildlife tourism, who established Shompole as a group venture with the local Maasai people. Named for the 1 550-metre mountain (*shompole* means 'place of red ochre') on the Kenya–Tanzania border, the lodge is surrounded by the 56 000-hectare Shompole Group Ranch. The holding ranch is Maasai owned and functions as a dispersal area for wildlife and a buffer zone to human settlement.

There's a lot to do, from day and night drives through the game-rich plains and mountain-biking along the edge of the escarpment to visits to the local Maasai market or walks at Lake Natron, breeding ground of East Africa's two million flamingos. Even an early-morning lie-in can be rewarding. While in my bed soaking up the sunrise, I was startled by vervet monkey alarm calls and was treated to the sight of a shy male leopard creeping below my deck to have a drink at the natural spring below

The main lounge and dining area at Main Shompole.

The suites at Little Shompole are built on stilts above the vegetation.

Lanterns light the path to Little Shompole's main building.

Main Shompole's raised dining area.

A guided walk with wildebeest.

While in my bed soaking up the sunrise, I...was treated to the sight of a *shy male leopard* creeping below my deck

details

When to go
Shompole is open all year. October and November are the hottest months; April and May are wet.

How to get there
A private charter flight takes 30 minutes from Jomo Kenyatta International Airport, and the lodge offers a shared charter flight three times a week.

Who to contact
Tel. (+254-20) 88 3331/2 or e-mail *reservations@theartofventures.com*

tropic air
nanyuki, kenya

Only by flying low across Kenya's physically diverse landscape can one truly appreciate the scale of its wild beauty. Tropic Air, with its knowledgeable pilots and well-maintained aircraft, provides the most unforgettable way to traverse this exceptional country.

Finding a secluded spot on the sandy bank to land the helicopter added a *buzz of excitement*

Our helicopter sped across the Laikipia plateau, through the rising sun towards Batian and Nelion, the snow-capped peaks of Mount Kenya. We skirted the slopes, where deep blue, icy tarns and sparkling waterfalls caught my eye. The pilot, Ben Simpson, descended and landed gently at the edge of Lake Alice. A champagne breakfast emerged from the Eurocopter and, high above the plains, we tucked in. At almost 3 900 metres, Lake Alice is known for its rainbow trout, and I couldn't resist trying my hand at a bit of fly-fishing. Conceding defeat, I boarded again and we headed north-west along the Ewaso N'giro River, over herds of elephants to the great Ol Ololokwe Mountain, one of the most striking landmarks in northern Kenya. Standing 1 000 metres above the flat plains, Ol Ololokwe is accessible only by foot or helicopter. A sheer rock face makes this flat-topped mountain both unique and identifiable from great distances. At its summit is a mist forest with giant cycads and superb birdlife, including Kenya's largest nesting colonies of Rüppell's vultures.

Leaving Ol Ololokwe, we flew along the banks of the Ewaso N'giro River, where the spring water flows over lava rock, and doum palms grow in clumps. Finding a secluded spot on the sandy bank to land the helicopter added a buzz of excitement, and stepping out into the cooling water was an experience second to none. For me, it was the perfect 40th birthday celebration.

Located on the equator in the heart of Kenya, Tropic Air was established in the mid-1990s by Kenyan-born Jamie Roberts. The company operates five aircraft, ranging from two-passenger Cessna 182s to a 12-passenger Cessna Caravan, plus two Eurocopters, which provide an even closer view of the landscape. The seven pilots have a combined 40 000 flying hours to their credit and are, in addition, knowledgeable about the country's history, landscape and wildlife. Tropic Air operates between lodges and camps located in Kenya's national parks and reserves – and more secret destinations too – enabling visitors to make the most of their visit and avoid the hazardous roads and vast distances, while experiencing a bird's-eye view of the spectacular scenery.

PREVIOUS SPREAD Picnicking on Ol Ololokwe Mountain.

THIS SPREAD The helicopter lands on a sandbar in the Ewaso N'giro River, where guests refresh themselves beneath a waterfall.

Flying past mist-veiled Mount Kenya.

A herd of elephants at the Ewaso N'giro River.

Mount Kenya's snow-capped peaks.

Ol Ololokwe's giant cycads.

details

Who to contact
Tel. (+254-62) 3 2890/1 or e-mail *tropic@africaonline.co.ke*

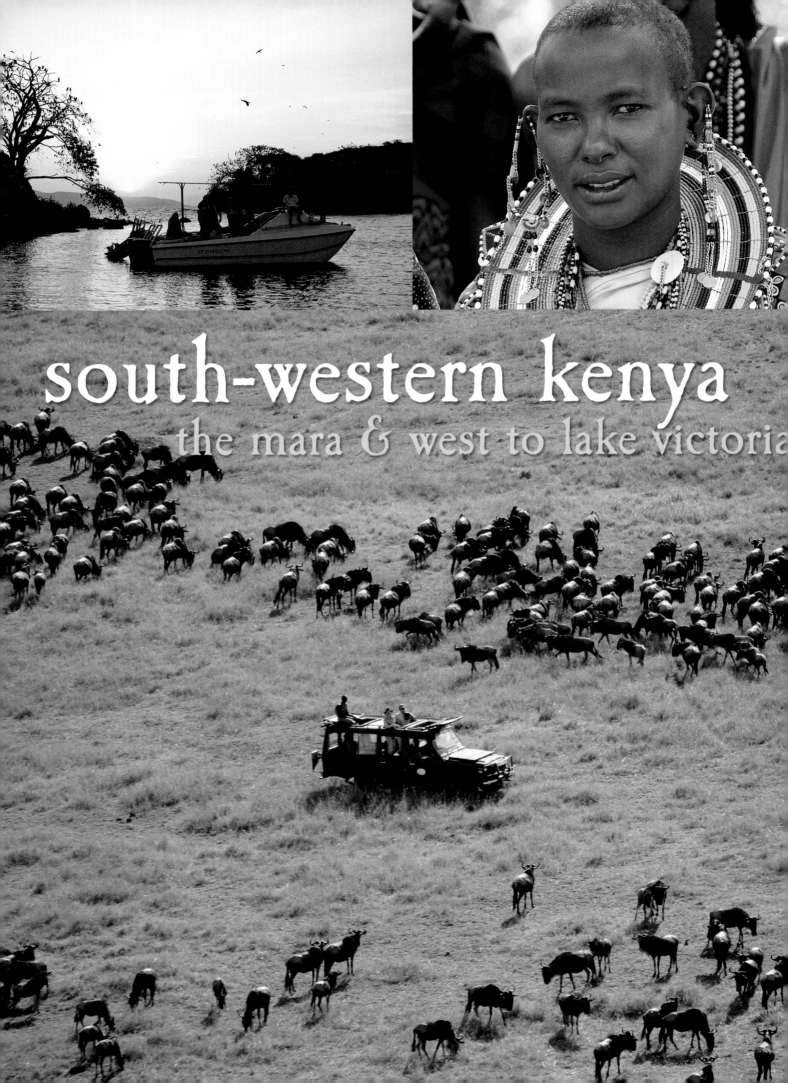

south-western kenya
the mara & west to lake victoria

For many people, the Masai Mara National Reserve, along with the adjacent Serengeti in Tanzania, encapsulates the African safari experience. Not surprisingly, it is the most visited of Kenya's wildlife reserves, especially during the migration, when guest-laden safari vehicles throng the banks of the Mara to watch the huge wildebeest herds as they cross the river. By contrast, Kenya west of the Mara is little visited by tourists, yet this lovely region embraces gems such as Kakamega Forest and magnificent Lake Victoria.

Wildebeest migration, Masai Mara National Reserve, Kenya

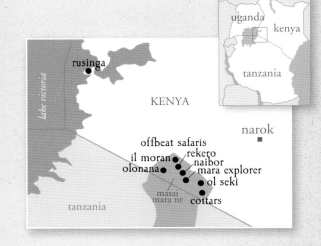

cottars 1920s safari camp

masai mara national reserve

Owned by a family that has
been in the safari industry
for 80 years, Cottars offers
a wildlife experience in the
grand old style.

'This area is *just as I enjoyed it* with my dad...
It's the Mara without the rush and the traffic jams'

PREVIOUS SPREAD A large canvas bath is filled beneath the stars.

THIS SPREAD The suites are spacious, with dressing rooms and *en-suite* bathrooms.

Giraffes lollop across the grassland.

Sundowners in the wilderness.

The walls may be canvas, but the interior is sheer comfort, colonial-style.

Relics of yesteryear.

Leaving the busy eastern Masai Mara National Reserve to the phalanxes of tourist-filled minibuses, we headed east towards the Olentoroto Hills, through thick euclea and acacia woodlands, past crystal-clear streams lined with yellowwood and giant fig trees, and across dry riverbeds. I felt like a true adventurer as we rocked across the plains, and envied the lives of Calvin and Louise Cottar, who operate an exclusive safari company in a rarely visited area of the Masai Mara. Registered in 1919 by Charles Cottar, the company is the oldest of its kind in Africa and has been passed from generation to generation. Calvin, the current incumbent, is Charles's great-grandson.

Our destination is Cottars 1920s camp, an exclusive and private concession neighbouring Loliondo Game Control Area and Serengeti National Park. The Cottars' dictum has always been to provide flexible safaris in wilderness areas that are off the beaten track, and Calvin follows this ethos passionately. 'This area is just as I enjoyed it with my dad, Glen. It's the Mara without the rush and the traffic jams.'

Emerging from an area of red crystalline rocks and thorny acacias, we reached the base of a forest-smothered hill. Black-and-white colobus monkeys chorused a greeting. Ahead of us lay a serene, white-canvassed camp, recalling a bygone era when safaris were unrushed, elegant and oozed romance.

I was escorted to my quarters, one of eight enormous tents decorated with original Cottars 1920s safari paraphernalia, from pith helmets and buffalo horns to framed portraits, bronze statues and voluminous travelling chests. The tents are well spaced, with dressing rooms and *en-suite* bathrooms with old-fashioned showers and flushing toilets. A rocking chair on the canopied veranda was the perfect viewing spot for panoramic views of the northern Serengeti and the eastern Mara, and of the great wildebeest migration which arrives in this region in July.

Activities are numerous and, at an additional cost (well worth it!), Calvin Cottar himself is available to lead safaris. There's little about life in the bush that Calvin, who has been voted one of the best guides in Kenya, does not know. The other guides, vetted and trained by Calvin, are also excellent.

There are game drives and walks ranging in duration from two hours to 10 days, the latter combined with overnight adventure camping. I opted for a one-day variation. After an early-morning call, my guide Douglas and I set off into the bush, where he led me close to a herd of 25 Masai giraffes. Then breakfast was served beneath a shady sausage-tree. Afterwards, a vintage wood-panelled safari vehicle ferried me through hills and valleys, where I spotted, amongst numerous other game, bushbuck in the trees and majestic buffalo.

In the evening, dinner was set up in a dry riverbed. There, accompanied by flickering candlelight and haunting tunes played on an old gramophone, I enjoyed an excellent meal on fine china. I felt I'd been thrown into a time warp. And it didn't end there – back at my tent, a large canvas bath had been prepared on my veranda. I ordered a large cognac, settled back into the hot water and contemplated the starry African night.

details

When to go
The camp is open all year. The annual wildebeest migration is present in the area from mid-July to the end of October, when conditions are cool and dry. The rains are heaviest in April, May and November.

How to get there
Private charter flights can be taken to Cottars's private airstrip. Air Kenya has scheduled flights to nearby Keekorok Lodge airstrip; Safarilink has a service to and from Nairobi and Tropic Air flies to and from northern Kenya. Flights are also available from Mombasa.

Who to contact
Tel. (+254-20) 88 3681, (+254-20) 88 3696/98, (+254-733) 77 3377 or (+254-720) 65 2976. E-mail *info@cottarsafaris.com* or go to *www.cottars.com*

il moran camp
masai mara national reserve

On the banks of the Mara River is a camp redolent with the atmosphere of the original hunting safaris.

Il Moran offers not only game drives, but also *walking safaris, fishing trips* and balloon flights over the reserve

Landing at Musiara Airstrip was like arriving in the Garden of Eden. To the south, wildebeest herds swarmed across the plains; to the west, elephants, water-buck and buffalo were feeding and bathing in the Musiara Marsh; to the east, a group of game-viewing vehicles had gathered around a small stream where a pride of lions with small cubs rested; and to the north, a group of hippos lay basking in the sun around a large waterhole.

Simon Siminye greeted me with a broad Kenyan smile. He has worked for the Governors' Camp organisation for 25 years, and is now one of the head guides based at Il Moran, my destination. Driving from the airstrip in an open Land Rover through the animals, I asked him, 'Is it always this way?' 'Yes,' was his answer, 'the marsh is a natural magnet to wildlife throughout the year. However, from July to October their numbers swell by the thousands, when the migration arrives from the Serengeti in search of fresh grazing.' It was already late October, so I was lucky to catch this spectacle.

This marshy Musiara area in the north-west Masai Mara National Reserve is where the owners of Governors' Camp established their first lodge in 1972, on the site of the exclusive retreat used by Kenya's colonial governors. Today Governors' Camp has six properties – four in the reserve, one at Lake Victoria and another on the shores of Lake Naivasha to the north-east. Il Moran is concealed in a private forest on the edge of the plains, with the Mara River flowing on its doorstep. Its name means 'warrior' in the Maasai language, an individual who stands out from the rest of the tribe, explained Simon. As the smallest and most luxurious of the Governors' portfolio of camps, Il Moran is certainly deserving of its appellation.

Here the atmosphere of the original safari hunting camps has been recreated with 10 cavernous canvas tents spread spaciously along the river. Like the others, my tent had a king-sized bed carved from fallen, ancient, gnarled olive trees. The *en-suite* bathroom was also fit for royalty, with a large Victorian bath, a shower, 'his' and 'hers' vanity basins, a flush toilet and a bidet. Lighting is powered by kerosene and gas. Outside, the capacious veranda offered views of shy bushbuck, dozing crocodiles and lazy hippos. Lured by the comfortable seating, I settled back to watch the birds, and was rewarded with sightings of Ross's and Schalow's turacos, green twinspots flitting in the undergrowth and large black-and-white-casqued horn-bills perched atop the giant strangler figs.

Afterwards, in the dining tent, I tucked into a delicious dinner, with complimentary wine, while enjoying the view of the river. For an additional cost, I could have enjoyed a candlelit dinner deep in the bush, as no doubt Kenya's early governors did.

Il Moran offers not only game drives, but also specialist walking safaris, fishing trips to Lake Victoria and balloon flights over the reserve. Floating gently above the plains at dawn is the perfect start to any day, especially when a champagne breakfast awaits your landing.

PREVIOUS SPREAD Ballooning across the game-rich Mara plains.

The tents combine rough-hewn wooden furniture, Persian rugs and antiques.

THIS SPREAD No expense has been spared to provide guests with luxurious accommodation.

Il Moran has 10 tents tucked beneath the ancient trees.

A lucky find! Cheetahs are rarely seen on game drives.

Small family groups of elephants enjoy the lush vegetation of the Musiara Marsh area.

Zebras gallop across the grassland in a thunder of hooves and a cloud of dust.

details

When to go
Il Moran is open all year.

How to get there
There is a return flight from Nairobi to Musiara Airstrip twice daily, with scheduled flights from other airports in Kenya. Arranged road transfers to the camp take 15 minutes. Il Moran is a six-hour drive from Nairobi.

Who to contact
Tel. Governors' Camp on (+254-20) 273 4000/5, fax (+254-20) 273 4023/4, e-mail *reservations@governorscamp.com* or go to *www.governorscamp.com*

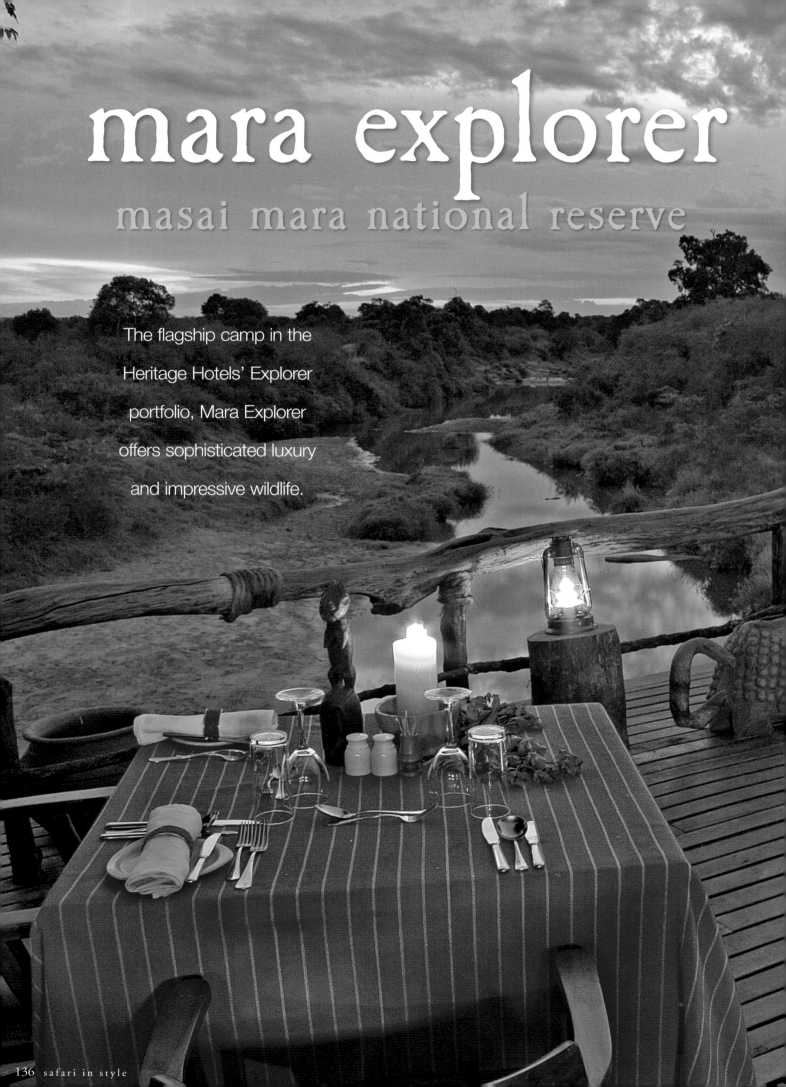

mara explorer

masai mara national reserve

The flagship camp in the
Heritage Hotels' Explorer
portfolio, Mara Explorer
offers sophisticated luxury
and impressive wildlife.

PREVIOUS SPREAD Dinner is served in a romantic setting overlooking the Talek River.

THIS SPREAD Monkeys and birds abound in the dense riverine forest.

A lone cheetah on the plains.

Game drives reveal treasures such as this pride of lions.

The wild outdoors is right on your doorstep.

A bathtub on the veranda ensures uninterrupted game-viewing.

The word 'explorer' evokes manly adventures and remote, untouched places. So staying at Mara Explorer camp in its concealed location made me feel like David Livingstone. After just one game drive with professional safari guide Paul Kirui, I was ready to call the area the predator capital of the world. We'd left at the crack of dawn after hearing noisy evidence of animal activity in the night. Just five minutes from the camp, we were greeted by the sight of a zebra killed by a pride of lions, and a vociferous group of 15 spotted hyaenas who were trying to drive them off. I watched entranced as a royal battle ensued, with the hyaenas emerging victorious and each running off with a share of the zebra remains.

Mara Explorer is located right in the centre of the Masai Mara National Reserve, with its 10 tents well-spaced and partially concealed by riverine forest on a bend in the Talek River. My tent had a huge double bed, hand-carved mahogany furniture and lots of memorabilia in the safari explorer style, including old prints, tin trunks and wooden chests. Although the camp itself is sheltered by the trees, it is in a core animal zone and is a natural magnet for loads of wildlife. Herbivores from the great grassy plains are drawn to the area by its mixed vegetation, mineral licks and water. In their wake come the predators and scavengers.

Leaving the kill site, we headed south to the great Burungat Plains. Paul's eagle-sharp eyes quickly spotted a mother cheetah with three large cubs hunting in the tall grass. I held my breath as the mother jumped onto the bonnet of our vehicle. As we watched her using us as a vantage point from which to spot prey, Paul explained that this was the famous cheetah, Kike, star of *Big Cat Diary*, filmed by the BBC.

We stopped for breakfast from a well-stocked picnic hamper provided by the camp's kitchen staff, and then explored further afield. With its central location, Mara Explorer allows you to access all the reserve's best wildlife areas.

Back at the camp, we sat down to dinner, hosted by the ever-attentive Mariana, who takes special care of all her guests. Our Maasai waiter served us smoothly and efficiently, and the food was fresh and delicious.

For me, one of the camp's best features was the extravagant, claw-foot bathtub on my balcony (each tent has one). There, while sipping champagne and soaking in bubbles, I watched elephants feeding and drinking in the river below, while being serenaded by honking hippos.

while sipping champagne and *soaking in bubbles*, I watched elephants feeding in the river below

details

When to go
Mara Explorer is a year-round destination. June to September is the best time to view the wildebeest migration. Big cats can be seen during the rest of the year.

How to get there
Charter flights transfer passengers to Mara Explorer's private airstrip.

Who to contact
Tel. (+254-20) 444 6651/7929/3404. E-mail *sales@heritagehotels.co.ke* or go to *www.heritage-eastafrica.com*

naibor camp
masai mara
national reserve

Sister camp to ultra-chic Shompole, Naibor combines modern safari style

with a rich wildlife and far-reaching benefits for the local community.

PREVIOUS SPREAD A game drive reveals an elephant at the edge of the riverine forest.

THIS SPREAD A double tent at Naibor, with fig-wood furniture and crisp bedding.

Hot coals are placed in the tents at night to keep the chill at bay.

Convivial evenings are spent in the dining and sitting-room tent.

Lunch is served!

Mountain-biking across the Mara plains is done under the watchful eye of an armed guard.

I was keen to see Naibor Camp as its designer, Anthony Russell, was responsible for the creation of Shompole. There, on the edge of the Nguruman Escarpment, this veteran of wildlife tourism had established a super-stylish lodge in a venture that included and benefited the local Maasai people. The principle behind Naibor, now under the ownership of Nigel Archer, was similar – style, comfort, wildlife and social responsibility.

After driving across open plains dotted with acacia trees and quartz-ite hills in the heart of the Masai Mara National Reserve, we entered a beautiful riverine forest. There, sheltered and private, were stylish pale-khaki canvas and white mesh tents, and I knew that the camp would live up to expectations. And, being just minutes away from some of the best-known wildebeest crossing sites, Naibor offers everything a safari enthusiast could need.

The word *naibor* means simplicity and space in Kiswahili, and that's exactly what has been achieved. Here, on the banks of the Talek River, the sweeping tents (six doubles and two twins) are stylishly furnished with light fig-wood furniture, sparkling white linen, soft drapery and vivid splashes of orange, lime green and yellow. The beds are king-sized, the chairs comfortable and the three-metre-wide private verandas offer the perfect spots to lounge on a day bed and watch the game go by. The tents themselves offer panoramic views and, lying in my bed one morning at sunrise while enjoying a cup of aromatic Kenyan coffee, I watched a herd of elephants lumber down to the river to drink, their passage accompanied by a chorus of birds. It was a magical moment. Resident hippos also provide constant entertainment.

There's a lot to do at Naibor and activities are arranged according to the wishes of the guests. The camp itself is in the central Mara plains, where game drives reveal wildlife at its uninterrupted best. I could have taken part in an all-day walk, with a bush breakfast and picnic lunch, hunted for honey or gone mountain-biking in a nearby conservancy, taken a balloon ride across the plains or even visited Lake Victoria for the day. I opted for a game drive and left with a guide early one morning, at first light. We encountered herds of elephants, buffalo, giraffes and an abundance of other plains game before heading back to camp with a keen appetite for breakfast. Here, the wildebeest migration takes place from July to October, depending on the rains. On their heels are the resident leopards, whose rasping territorial calls at night announced their presence and disturbed my sleep. Visits to a Maasai cultural village can also be arranged.

Each night the guests gathered in the dining tent to share their day's sightings and enjoy the superb meals created with locally grown pro-duce, including interesting spices and herbs.

Later, when I retired, a smiling Maasai steward brought hot water in buckets to fill my shower. The temperature was perfect – just like the camp.

The word *naibor* means simplicity and space, and that's exactly what has been achieved

details

When to go
Naibor Camp is closed in April, May and November.

How to get there
Naibor is close to both scheduled and chartered airstrips, with Ol Kiombo being the closest. From Narok, it's a 90-minute trip by road.

Who to contact
Tel. (+254-20) 8 83331/2, e-mail *info@theartofventures.com* or go to *www.theartofventures.com*

offbeat
safaris
throughout kenya

When the only sound between you and the
wilderness is the beat of your horse's hooves,
you know you're on a safari second to none.

Riding on horseback through big-game country brings another dimension to the word safari. My steed was a home-bred, well-schooled polo pony. On its back, I felt at one with the environment, and far superior to those whose game-viewing was conducted from a clattering diesel-powered vehicle.

In addition, there is no better person to lead you through the wilds on horseback than Tristan Voorspuy. Having grown up with horses in Kenya and spent six years in the British Household Cavalry, his equestrian knowledge and experience is excellent. In the 1980s he returned to Kenya, where he immersed himself in horseback guiding. In 1990, he started his own company, Offbeat Safaris, which now operates throughout Kenya, from the ranches of Laikipia to the Loita–Mara in the southwest and along the Tanzanian border between Amboseli National Park and the Chyulu Hills.

The safaris are available in a number of permutations, tailor-made for small or larger groups and for periods of up to 14 days. You can stay in mobile camps or combine horseback and conventional safaris with accommodation in luxury tented camps.

I began my trip at Deloraine, a basalt mansion in the grand colonial style built in 1920 by early settler Lord Francis Scott on 2 000 hectares on the lower slopes of Londiani Mountain, near Nakuru. This is the home of Tristan and his wife Lucinda, who have restored the house and offer a luxurious base or starting point for those on their way to the Masai Mara National Reserve. Eighty horses are kept on the estate, and there are cross-country and polo facilities as well as a tennis court and a swimming pool.

Having recovered from my jetlag and made the acquaintance of the horses, I set off with Tristan to the Masai Mara to begin our short safari. There is no other place in the world where one can ride on horseback alongside thousands of wildebeest and zebras, and trotting through the Mara ecosystem was truly special. A tented camp had been placed on top of the Siria Escarpment, which forms the western boundary of the Masai Mara. Using this camp as a base, we rode into the Mara Conservancy, with savanna and animals as far as the eye could see. After riding along the top of the plateau, we then descended the escarpment on foot onto the balanites plains, with their completely different vegetation.

On the second day we descended onto the plains again, heading east and crossing the Mara River under the watchful eyes of a pod of hippos curious about these zebras without stripes. We entered the land of the Maasai, where Tristan's excellent team had moved the camp onto the banks of the Mara River. That night, beneath the star-studded canopy of the African sky, I reflected on my good fortune in being able to ride. Horseback safaris are not for novices; one has to be proficient in the saddle to be able to gallop away from trouble should the need arise.

PREVIOUS SPREAD Good riding ability is essential when exploring big-game country on horseback.

THIS SPREAD Few people have experienced the unique feeling of galloping across the African savanna.

Deloraine nestles on the forested lower slopes of Londiani Mountain.

Guests at Deloraine have included British royalty, including the Queen Mother as a young bride.

Taking a breather.

Horseback safaris allow an intimate insight into plains game.

details

When to go
Riding safaris can be taken all year.

How to get there
Deloraine is a three-hour drive from Nairobi or a 50-minute charter flight from Jomo Kenyatta International Airport. The Mara is a six-hour drive from Nairobi, and is serviced by both charter flights and a twice-daily service with Air Kenya.

Who to contact
Tel. (+254-51) 34 3122/3123 or (+254-720) 46 1300, e-mail *offbeat@africaonline.co.ke* or *sarah@offbeatsafaris.com*, or go to *www.offbeatsafaris.com*

olonana
camp
greater mara

Tucked beneath the magnificent Siria Escarpment, Olonana is at the forefront of eco-friendly wildlife tourism.

But the deceptively simple exterior belies the *luxury within*, as I was surprised to discover

PREVIOUS SPREAD The tents at Olonana Camp are a sophisticated refuge from the wild outdoors.

The camp is partially concealed by pristine forest on the banks of the Mara River.

THIS SPREAD Maasai villagers provide evening entertainment.

A lioness surveys the grassland terrain.

Hippos wallow obligingly beneath the camp.

A game drive reveals a herd of elephants.

The sitting room.

Olonana was the younger of two sons of Chief Oloiboni Mpatiany, the spiritual leader of Kenya's Maasai people during the 19th century. After his father died, Olonana became the paramount chief of the Maasai until his death in 1911. He was a greatly respected leader and here, on the banks of the Mara River, a safari camp has been named in his honour.

The Maasai influence is felt from the moment you arrive at the camp, with its entrance built like a traditional house. The main lodge is clad in mud and dung with woven croton branches. But the deceptively simple exterior belies the luxury within, as I was surprised to discover. Originally established by South African adventurer Kingsley Holgate as a Maasai cultural centre, Olonana became a luxury tented camp in 1999, and the cultural village was relocated close by.

I was shown to my tent by Morris the butler, who led me through pristine riverine forest along the banks of the Mara River. The Olonana tents are huge, each being over 10 metres long with twin queen-sized beds carefully positioned to give you a view of the river while lying back on your pillows. Large phonolitic boulders litter the opposite bank, a reminder of the volcanic activity that occurred many millions of years ago. Morris pointed out that, if I was lucky, I might see the famous leopard called Zawadi who, with her cub, often relaxes on the rocks across the river in front of the camp.

Olonana lies on the western border of the Masai Mara National Reserve, with the huge Siria, or Oloololo, Escarpment behind the camp and the Mara River in front. Most game drives are conducted in the western section of the Mara reserve, but this is also excellent walking territory. Accompanied by expert ornithologist Elly Gathungu and an armed Maasai warrior, we started hiking up the escarpment, and I was lucky enough to see some of the Mara's specials – a Chandler's mountain reedbuck, a family of klipspringers and a long-billed pipit. Once at the top, with Olonana way beneath us, we had uninterrupted views of the entire Mara plains. I found game-walking a welcome diversion to spending a day in a vehicle, distanced from the animals.

I also visited the local Maasai village, which Olonana supports, to observe the cultural heritage of these warriors and pastoralists.

One of the highlights for me was the huge effort that has been undertaken to make Olonana Camp a truly eco-friendly camp. Elly took me on a tour of the sophisticated wetlands system that purifies all the waste water from the camp. This wetland also provides a natural sanctuary for many animal species, from butterflies and insects to birds, frogs and reptiles. Best of all, I thought, is that the water taken from the Mara is returned cleaner than when it was removed.

details

When to go
Olonana is open all year.

How to get there
Charter flights transport passengers to Kichwa Tembo airstrip, some 15 minutes' drive from camp. There are also twice-daily scheduled flights.

Who to contact
Tel. (+254-20) 695 0002/0244 or e-mail *kenya@sanctuarylodges.com*

ol seki mara camp

masai mara national reserve

A chorus of wildlife, from snorting wildebeest to howling hyaenas and roaring lions, is the permanent soundtrack of this unspoilt corner of the Masai Mara.

A guest at Ol Seki described the camp in a short, three-letter word – WOW! And that was the exact word that sprung to mind when I first saw it from the air. The combination of isolated location, its situation on dramatic rocks looking east and west across the land of the Maasai and its unusual 12-sided tents on wooden platforms was striking. The Ol Seki Mara Camp may have many competitors in the Masai Mara National Reserve, but it is certainly in a class of its own.

It was some months later that I finally realised my desire to visit the camp, one of the newest in the region. It was developed by the Allan family, who are passionate about the local ecology and environment. Sue Allan, with over 36 years of safari experience to her credit, and her son Jan and daughter-in-law Erin have designed and created a camp that combines personal charm with the ultimate in luxurious accommodation.

Sue was there in person to meet me. She showed me around and it soon became evident that she has made this small six-tented camp her second home, and it shows. It oozes attention to detail, from the carefully designed, spacious round tents to the fully equipped, open-plan kitchen and breakfast bar. There's also an elegant dining tent and a seductively comfortable, well-stocked library tent for quiet reflection and a good read.

Traditionally, the olseki, or sandpaper, tree symbolises peace, harmony and wealth – the very essence of the camp. Ol Seki is surrounded by succulents, and acacia and olseki trees, which

I was tempted by the *glorious views* of the Il Sabukioi River

grow naturally on these rocky outcrops. I was tempted by the glorious views of the Il Sabukioi River and the valley, and relaxed on the wooden veranda watching the wildlife. There is a wonderful, uncrowded sense of Africa in this corner of the Mara, with all its plains game, lions, cheetahs, wild dogs, jackals, elephants and buffalo. The richness of the animal life is complemented by the paucity of people.

Ol Seki is a member of the Ecotourism Society of Kenya and has won accolades for its environmental programme. I was impressed by their new leaf-and-cow-dung fuel briquette machine, which has been given to the local Maasai community and developed in an effort to prevent the local trees being felled for fires. Community involvement is very much a part of their programme.

The guides here are all professional. Betty, a new graduate from the Koyaki Guide Training School, spoke enthusiastically of her heritage and her love of her new career. I took a guided walk with the local Il Ndorobo hunter-gatherer, Letilet, to his old home, a cave in an overhang below the camp. Now a game-spotter for the camp, Letilet's traditional knowledge and tales of his hunting days are not to be missed. Like the camp, they are a rare and wonderful find.

PREVIOUS SPREAD The tents are built on wooden platforms.

The bedrooms are luxuriously decorated with locally produced furniture and fine linens.

THIS SPREAD From your suite, you can read or lose yourself in the limitless vista.

In the guest book, visitors leave glowing, even artistic, impressions of their stay.

You may be in the middle of nowhere, but the food is sophisticated and delicious.

The elegant dining room.

A giraffe threesome.

details

When to go
Ol Seki Mara Camp is open from December to March and from June to November.

How to get there
From Nairobi's Wilson Airport, daily morning and afternoon scheduled flights to nearby Siana airstrip and charters into Koiyaki airstrip take about 40 minutes. By road from Nairobi, the journey is some five to six hours via Narok.

Who to contact
Tel. (+254-20) 89 1190/89 0375, e-mail *info@olseki.com* or *admin@olseki.com* or go to *www.olseki.com*

rekero camp
masai mara national reserve

'Far from the madding crowd' aptly describes this small tented camp in the central Masai Mara National Reserve.

As Rekero is a seasonal camp, it has no fences, so *animals often come to visit*

In 1995 I discovered a special place in the central Masai Mara National Reserve. The site of a long abandoned ranger post, it was situated along the banks of the Talek River near its confluence with the Mara River. A thick grove of trees stood on the northern bank, to the south lay a vast open plain. Forty kilometres to the east, mass tourism flourished. Yet this place could not have been more wild or remote.

Now, 10 years later, I am standing in exactly the same spot. Little has changed. The area is still isolated, the grove of trees has not been felled for a large cumbersome lodge. Instead, tucked beneath the branches, a small exclusive luxury mobile camp has been erected. It is lunch-time, and the grassy plains to the south of the river are heaving with wildebeest on the move. Thousands upon thousands of these beasts are pushing down towards the river below us. I am sitting at an open-air lunch table beneath a giant pepper-bark tree. Before me is a sumptuous home-cooked meal, across the river is the teeming game.

Wildebeest have been crossing the Talek River at this particular spot for years and they're getting ready to take the plunge again. Suddenly the first animal leaps into the water and, for the next two hours, I am treated to one of the greatest wildlife spectacles in the world.

Rekero Camp is set up seasonally to view the best plains' action. It caters for up to 14 guests in seven well-spaced tents on the banks of the Talek. All offer wonderful views of the river and the southern plains, yet the camp is invisible from all angles except above. The tents are spacious, with comfortable beds, locally produced furniture and *en-suite* bathrooms. There are flush toilets, and showers fed with piping-hot water via canvas buckets.

As Rekero is a seasonal camp, it has no fences, so animals often come to visit. But there's no need for alarm, as local Maasai warriors will escort you to and from your tents. And the opportunity to experience nature at such close range makes this an exceptional wild adventure.

The Beaton family arrived in Africa in 1889 and were pioneers in Kenya's conservation movement. The family's work is continued by Gerard and Rainee Beaton who, along with their partner Jackson Ole Looseyia, own and host Rekero Camp. Their team of professional local safari guides and camp crew has worked together for years, combining cultural heritage and bush savvy with guiding skills taught at the training school pioneered by Ron Beaton, Gerard's father.

I took a safari drive in a customised 4x4. Animal-watching is hungry work, and at midday we fell upon Rainee's superb picnic lunch. Later, Jackson confided, 'If people don't love it here, they won't be happy anywhere. I love the peace, freedom and hospitality of the Masai Mara. Part of me stays here whenever I leave. I'm proud to show guests everything and I want them to learn as much as possible about Kenya and its wildlife.'

PREVIOUS SPREAD Milllions of wildebeest cross the Mara plains every year in search of fresh grazing.

THIS SPREAD Game drives at sunset offer unique photographic opportunities.

A highlight of the day is sharing tales of the day's sightings aound the evening camp fire.

Each tent's private veranda offers wide views across the grassy plains.

Local fabrics and *en-suite* bathrooms ensure a comfortable stay.

Maasai guides lead visitors across the Talek River.

details

When to go
Rekero operates from June to October and December to March.

How to get there
Air Kenya and Safari Link operate twice daily schedule services from Wilson Airport to nearby Ol Kiombo airstrip. Private charters can also be arranged.

Who to contact
E-mail *rekerocamp@africaonline.co.ke* or visit *www.rekerocamp.com*

rusinga island lodge

lake victoria

A tranquil island retreat, Rusinga Lodge is the ideal location to recharge

your batteries after a long flight or a challenging East African safari.

As I entered the front door of Rusinga Island Lodge, I was handed a chilled, scented cloth. Then, as I passed through the reception area, I was struck by the sight of a huge fig tree and the largest lake in Africa. I stood beneath the tree for a moment, dwarfed by its magnitude and overwhelmed by the 68 800-square-kilometre body of water that stretched to the west, south and north of the island. This is Lake Victoria, the second largest in the world and the source of the Nile River.

Rusinga Island lies on the eastern reaches of the lake. I'd just left the dry savanna plains of the Masai Mara National Reserve, some 40 minutes away by air, and the contrast couldn't have been more marked. Here lush subtropical vegetation and the sparkling water held a promise of lazy afternoons and somnolent tranquillity.

The lodge is owned by John Cars, an Englishman born in Uganda, whose father served as chief engineer on several of the East African Railways and Harbours' steamships that operated on the lake. It is after one of these ships, the *SS Rusinga*, that the island is named. John visited the island in 2001 on holiday and, as he says, 'I woke up on my birthday, walked out onto the veranda of my room and decided then and there to buy the lodge'. He took over in 2002 and has completely rebuilt it.

The eight cottages, each named after a local bird, have high thatched roofs. Spacious patios look out to lush gardens and the sparkling lake. A health spa with fully trained staff adds to the sense of pampering, and there is a swimming pool.

It was not only the lodge's facilities that appealed to me, but also the gracious hospitality of managers Wayne and Tanya and their team of highly competent local Luo staff. The individual needs of each guest are catered to. You could choose to take breakfast or lunch indoors or on the lawns, while dinners are served in Fish Eagle House, outside on the candlelit jetty or at the pool.

The huge fruiting fig trees and many flowering plants attract hosts of vibrantly coloured birds. There are over 300 species recorded, with several that occur only in western Kenya. I took a bird walk around the gardens with a guide, and saw a double-toothed barbet, black-headed gonolek, eastern grey plantain-eater and red-chested sunbirds. Even if you're not a birder, at Rusinga you will almost certainly become one. Other activities are various, with watersports, great fishing (especially for the giant-sized Nile perch) and sun-downer visits to nearby Bird Island. Ruma National Park is also accessible and worth a day trip to see some of Kenya's rarer species – Rothschild's giraffe, roan antelope, Jackson's hartebeest and oribi.

PREVIOUS SPREAD At Rusinga Island Lodge, a jetty stretches into Lake Victoria, the second largest lake in the world.

THIS SPREAD The lake is a rich source of food for the African fish-eagle.

The thatched suites have comfortable patios from which to relax and take in the view.

Well-appointed bedrooms ensure a good night's sleep.

A relaxing massage in a magnificent setting.

There's great fishing to be had in the lake.

lush subtropical vegetation and the *sparkling water* held a promise of lazy afternoons

details

When to go
Rusinga Island Lodge is open all year.

How to get there
Rusinga Island Lodge is a 15-minute flight from Kisumu; a 35-minute flight from the Masai Mara and 90 minutes from Nairobi. All flights are by private charter aircraft. The airstrip is adjacent to the lodge. From Kisumu, it takes three hours by road, ferry and the Mbita causeway.

Who to contact
Tel. (+254-20) 88 2028, e-mail *info@privatewilderness.com*.
Go to *www.rusinga.com* or *www.privatewilderness.com*

home of the gorilla
uganda

Bwindi Impenetrable Forest, Uganda

Bordered by the two main arms of the Great Rift Valley, Uganda is strikingly different from its eastern and southern neighbours. Here, the great savannas meet the tropical rainforests of western Central Africa. It is a verdant place, where crops thrive and the spectre of drought and starvation that often hangs over much of Africa recedes. When it comes to wildlife experiences, reserves such as Queen Elizabeth and Semliki are superb, but the star attraction is undoubtedly primates, with the chimpanzee and mountain gorilla reigning supreme.

apoka safari lodge
kidepo valley national park

Tucked into a remote, rugged corner of north-eastern Uganda, Apoka offers a greater variety of game than is found anywhere else in the country.

Hundreds of elephants streamed along the Narus River valley and lines of buffalo *stretched to the horizon*

PREVIOUS SPREAD Apoka's thatched roofs blend almost seamlessly with the rugged environment.

THIS SPREAD Armed guards lead visitors as close to the animals as possible.

A duo of lions pauses in the long grass.

Crisp bedlinen and mosquito drapes ensure a good night's sleep.

A refreshing dip and a glass of wine are the perfect end to a day on safari.

Apoka's many-windowed suites afford ever-changing views of the wilderness.

Hundreds of elephants streamed along the Narus River valley and lines of buffalo stretched to the horizon. In the distance the Lonyili Mountains were etched sharply against the sky as if hand-coloured in brown pastel. It was just after the first rains in northern Uganda and I was on a balcony of the brand-new Apoka Safari Lodge in an extremely isolated and beautiful wilderness area, wedged against the Sudanese border, called Kidepo Valley National Park.

Apoka is the newest lodge in the Uganda's Wild Places collection, created by the Uganda Safari Company (the others are Emin Pasha Hotel in Kampala and Semliki Lodge at the southern tip of Lake Albert) and typifies the company's ability to bring luxury to the wilds. Each of the 10 thatched, canvas-walled rooms has an *en-suite* bathroom, a king-sized bed and glorious private views.

From the thatched communal lounge on the slopes of a rocky koppie, I gazed across a small waterhole to the valley and the mountains beyond. A constant stream of animals arrived to drink. During the dry season, I was told, up to 1 000 buffalo are encamped outside the lodge, and it's quite common to spot prowling lions and cheetahs from the veranda.

Sausage-trees and fan-shaped borassus palms offer some cover on the open savanna plains of this 1 492-square-kilometre reserve, which begs to be explored on game drives and walking trails. Our guide took us close – but not too close – to a variety of large animals. Giraffes are notoriously curious and lumbered towards us for a closer look. The buffalo were less accommodating; as soon as they caught our scent they stampeded out of range with hammering hooves. We also surprised a pride of lions camped out on a rocky hill. A broad-maned male growled fiercely, and we retraced our steps with wildly beating hearts. 'There's nowhere else like this in Africa,' said our guide later as he led us along a necklace of lakes that had pooled in the river. 'It is totally remote and uncorrupted by tourism.'

The park contains a wealth of animals, including 86 mammal species, 28 of which occur nowhere else in the country. Among the more unusual species for me were Jackson's hartebeest, bohor reedbuck, Defassa waterbuck, Rothschild's giraffe, Günther's dik-dik, as well as patas and tantalus monkeys. One afternoon on a game drive we spotted an eagle on a clump of euphorbia. It most closely resembled a greater spotted eagle, which according to bird books is a species previously documented only in Sudan and Ethiopia. 'We keep finding birds that are not supposed to be here,' our guide said.

It's an exciting time for Kidepo – and for the local Karamajong people who have started to benefit from tourism. These tall, proud Nilotic people have had little contact with the outside world, and cattle still serve as their main currency. There are plans for guided tours to nearby Karenga Village, and one evening after dinner we were entertained with local songs and high-jumping dances as a taste of what's in store.

The Karamajong are also learning cooking skills from the chef at the Emin Pasha Hotel in Kampala. 'They had a long way to go,' he told me. 'When I arrived they were only good at cutting up cows!' Now their dishes include lobster, flown in from the coast.

details

When to go
The lodge is open all year.

How to get there
Apoka is a 90-minute flight from Entebbe International Airport. There are also plans to offer a direct service in and out of Kenya.

Who to contact
Tel. (+256-41) 25-1182, e-mail *info@wildplacesafrica.com* or go to *www.wildplacesafrica.com* or *www.safariuganda.com*

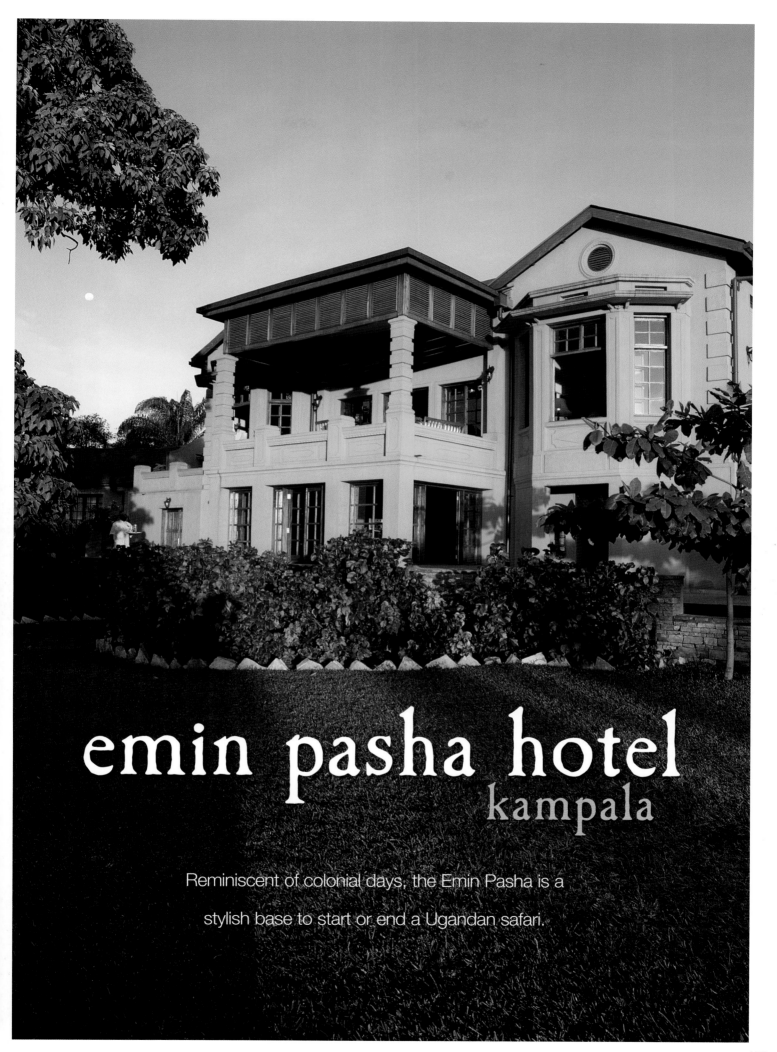

emin pasha hotel
kampala

Reminiscent of colonial days, the Emin Pasha is a

stylish base to start or end a Ugandan safari.

'We're on the equator, so we really try to *celebrate* that'

It was six in the evening. On the wide veranda of the Emin Pasha Hotel in Uganda's capital city of Kampala, a stylish mix of foreigners, travellers and business people were gathered for cocktails, fragrant espresso coffees and the sort of delectable cuisine you would expect to find in a European city. After a week of journeying through Uganda's spectacular landscapes and wild places, I tucked into a cold beer, a Caesar salad and, switching on my computer, sent some images home wirelessly.

Owners of the hotel Jonathan and Pamela Wright also own Wild Places, a collection of safari lodges which includes Apoka Lodge, Semliki Lodge and a ground-operating company called the Uganda Safari Company. They are setting new standards of accommodation in Uganda and helping the country to reach its much-needed tourist potential.

'Our safari clients were disappointed on previous visits to Kampala. Most of the accommodation lacked real character,' said Pamela. 'We wanted to change that. We drove past the derelict home on this site every day and figured that it offered an opportunity to create something that could hold its head up high in Africa.'

Now it's hard to imagine that the Emin Pasha was ever anything less than perfect. The original double-storey home has been completely refurbished. The reception rooms are resplendent with polished wooden floors, pots of flowers and original Ugandan artworks. Two wings accommodate the restaurant, a conference facility, lounging decks and 21 luxury rooms. *En-suite* bathrooms, satellite television, Internet connections and great views are standard, but each bedroom also has its own particular character. Mine was downstairs with a patio that opened into the lush, bird-filled tropical garden. There were neat lawns, tall trees and a sparkling swimming pool. 'We're on the equator, so we really try to celebrate that,' said Pamela.

During my stay, I rubbed shoulders with politicians, diplomats, pilots, a three-star US general and a great many others who all agreed that Pamela and Jonathan have found the right formula.

The dining was exquisite, thanks to Dan Evans – a Michelin-star-rated chef with a passion for a cooking style he describes as eclectic. 'When I was young, I knew that I wanted to be a chef,' he told me one morning as we scoured Kampala's vibrant markets in search of things fresh and delicious. 'I wrote to every three-star Michelin-rated chef in Europe and eventually camped outside the door of one of them; he finally agreed to give me a job.' He now trains the Emin Pasha kitchen staff, giving several Ugandan *sous-chefs* a chance to learn his craft.

White robes and red fez hats (standard garments for the waiters) were introduced to Uganda by the hotel's namesake, Emin Pasha, a late-19th-century German explorer, doctor and naturalist who escaped the Mahdi rebellion in the Sudan and took refuge in northern Uganda. Explorer Henry Morton Stanley was sent to track him down, and found him healthy, content and with no intention of leaving his new-found home. They celebrated with three bottles of champagne that had survived the journey with Stanley.

'That's just how I feel about Uganda,' said Pamela who clearly has no plans to return to her native Canada. Sitting on the veranda of the Emin Pasha, I knew just what she meant.

details

When to go
The Emin Pasha Hotel is open all year.

How to get there
The hotel is in the centre of Kampala, 40 minutes by road from Entebbe International Airport.

Who to contact
Tel. (+256-41) 23 6977/8/9, e-mail *info@eminpasha.com*, or go to *www.eminpasha.com* or *www.safariuganda.com*

gorilla forest camp
western uganda

Bwindi Impenetrable National Park is a Tarzan-like world of

steaming jungles, tropical birds and the impressive mountain gorilla.

PREVIOUS SPREAD A gorilla, one of Bwindi's troop of more than 300, peeps through the foliage.

Gorilla Forest Camp has a comfortable veranda from which guests can watch monkeys tumble and chatter in the surrounding trees.

THIS SPREAD Rwansigazi, the 40-year-old silverback leader of the Rushegura group of gorillas.

Numerous waterfalls occur in the tropical rainforest at Bwindi Impenetrable National Park.

Guests receive their pre-trek briefing.

Winding paths lead to the private chalets.

A view across the dense forest, home to 93 mammal species and more than 340 types of birds.

[Rwansigazi] stared hard, then *beat his muscled chest* in a thunderous display of authority

Swirling mists shroud the mountain slopes of Bwindi Impenetrable National Park – a 420-square-kilometre tropical rainforest reserve that forms the boundary between Uganda and the Democratic Republic of Congo. Here, tucked into the jungle, is Gorilla Forest Camp. All around, the trees are home to 93 types of mammal and 345 bird species, but it is famously known for its resident population of around 320 mountain gorillas. These, the largest of Africa's primates, reach up to 1.8 metres in height and occur only in the forest ecosystems of Rwanda, Zaire and Uganda. Bwindi is home to three groups of habituated gorillas – Rushegura, Habinyanja and Mubare. Daily permits are issued to just eight visitors per group, so there are never more than 24 trekkers inside the entire park.

The drive to Bwindi passes through the emerald-green, cultivated highlands of south-western Uganda. The park itself remains pristine and the treed slopes buzz with life. At the pre-trek briefing, the guides from Uganda Wildlife Authority introduced us to the dos and don'ts of dealing with gorillas, emphasising, 'Whatever you do, don't challenge the silverback – just keep very still and look down if he approaches you.' Thus warned, and covered from head to toe in the requisite long trousers, long-sleeved shirts, boots, gloves and wet-weather gear, we set off on our three-hour journey through stinging nettles, lianas and thick forest.

I had been allocated to the Rushegura group, whose 13 members are led by the 40-year-old silverback, Rwansigazi. The groups can be elusive, but we were lucky – just 20 minutes after setting out we were told that the troop was very close. We left our bags with the porters and, clutching our cameras, plunged into the forest. Then a large, fur-fringed black face peered through the undergrowth, and I saw my first gorilla. As she tilted her head, her big, gentle eyes looked at me kindly. Then the silverback male came into view. I have never seen a primate anything like Rwansigazi, who must have weighed nearly 200 kilograms. He stared hard, then beat his muscled chest in a thunderous display of authority that left both man and beast in no doubt about who was in charge.

Our allotted hour passed swiftly and we had to leave. Fortunately, the gorillas spent the rest of the day loitering in the vicinity of the lodge, giving us some unexpected viewing.

At Gorilla Forest Camp all meals and drinks are included, and we spent some lazy hours on the veranda, watching the monkeys. Wanting to see more of the forest, I signed up for the three-hour guided Waterfall Walk. We rambled beneath the canopy, crossing bridges over gurgling streams, until we reached a number of rushing falls, the largest of which was approximately 30 metres in height.

Heavy tropical rain fell that afternoon – as it often does in this part of the world – and we donned our ponchos and hurried back to the lodge. Tired and wet, we took wonderful steaming baths in our rooms, which have views of the forest, then gathered at the lodge for hot soup and bream. The coal heater beneath our table warmed our feet, and later we clambered into bed to discover thoughtfully provided hot-water bottles. I drifted to sleep to the now-familiar sound of a silverback beating his chest.

details

When to go
Gorilla Camp is open throughout the year.

How to get there
It's a 10-hour drive from Kampala to Bwindi, or you can fly directly to a small airstrip nearby.

Who to contact
Go to *www.thefarhorizons.com* or email *info@thefarhorizons.com*

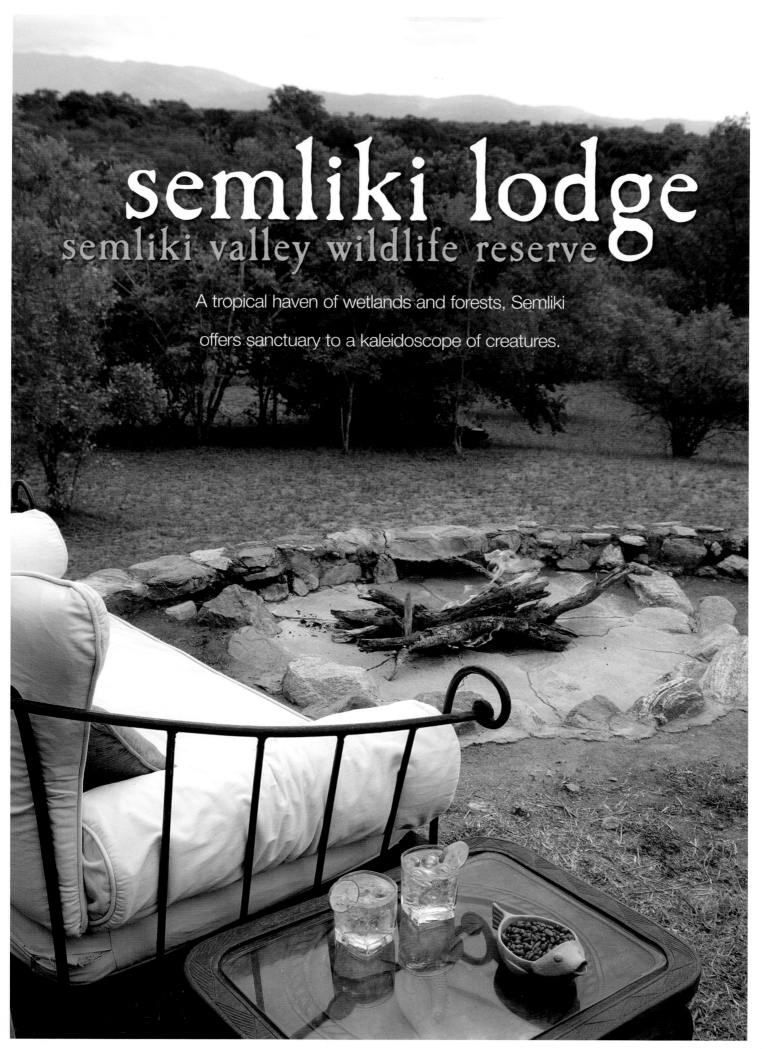

semliki lodge
semliki valley wildlife reserve

A tropical haven of wetlands and forests, Semliki

offers sanctuary to a kaleidoscope of creatures.

PREVIOUS SPREAD The dense forests at Semliki Valley Wildlife Reserve are home to more than 450 bird species, including numerous members of the weaver family.

In the evenings, a fire is lit in the grounds and the stage is set for pre-dinner drinks

THIS SPREAD Semliki's steep, thatched roof shelters a shady veranda.

There's a cool pool with views across the tangle of vegetation.

Numerous monkeys live in the forests.

Nature may prevail outdoors, but indoors the guest accommodation is welcoming and comfortable.

A game drive at Semliki.

We crossed a rickety rope bridge over the Wasa River, following the panicked call of a troop of monkeys. There, in a tangle of emerald vegetation, we saw the cause of their consternation – a yellow-and-black cat. It was not the longest leopard sighting of my life, nor the clearest, but tracking and finding one of Semliki Valley Wildlife Reserve's leopards on foot ranks among my sweetest nature experiences ever.

Semliki covers 550 square kilometres on the Western Rift Valley escarpment – a geological rampart that extends from Lake Albert southwards to Zambia's Luangwa Valley. The region has been declared an important conservation area by the World Conservation Union on account of its high biodiversity, and Semliki is smack in the middle of it, between the plunging escarpment and the rise of the Ruwenzori Mountains.

Proclaimed in 1932, Semliki, called Toro Game Reserve at the time, was home to black-maned lions and the highest concentration of Uganda kob in the country. Then, in the 1970s, civil war broke out and poaching decimated the game, reducing the kob numbers from 30 000 to just a few hundred.

Jonathan Wright, a Ugandan by birth, returned to the country in the mid-1990s to help the Uganda Wildlife Authority restore the park. 'Where else do you get lion and chimpanzees living together, three types of pigs, waterfalls that drop from the escarpment and both forest and savanna elephants?' he asked me. He established the Uganda Safari Company and, in 1997, Semliki Safari Lodge was built. Now the company, along with its newly formed partner, Wild Places, manages numerous lodges, including Apoka in the Kidepo Valley in the north-east.

You don't even have to stray from your veranda at Semliki Lodge to appreciate the sights. All the rooms, as well as the sitting and dining areas, overlook dense galleries of trees filled with chattering monkeys, low-flying turacos and multicoloured birds.

Semliki's eight tents each have a four-poster bed and a spacious *en-suite* bathroom. Our days began with a gentle knock on the door and a tray of fragrant Ugandan coffee and fresh muffins. Replete, we set out to explore the riparian forest, savanna, acacia woodlands, rainforest, wetlands and hardwood forests. This diverse habitat is home to more than 450 bird species, earning the reserve a place among the Important Bird Areas in Uganda.

Other Semliki specials include red river hogs, giant hogs, African golden cat, short-snouted crocodiles, forest and savanna elephants and chimpanzees. The University of Indiana has conducted a chimp research project here for some years and researchers have noted that the primates often feed in the open savanna in a bipedal fashion, fuelling speculation that they could reveal important clues about human evolution. If you're spending a few days at Semliki, you may be able to join the researchers on their forays into the park.

'We've been here for 10 years and have only seen the tip of it,' Jonathan told me. I spent just two nights at Semliki – hardly long enough to discover its many hidden secrets, but it was heartwarming to learn how the wildlife has recovered since the lodge was established and game patrols began. Kob numbers are up to 10 000, and we also saw 200-strong herds of buffalo. At night the roar of several Semliki lions reminded us that they, too, were back on patrol.

details

When to go
Semliki is open all year.

How to get there
The lodge is a four-and-a-half-hour drive from Kampala. It has its own landing strip for light aircraft.

Who to contact
E-mail *info@wildplacesafrica.com* or go to *www.wildplacesafrica.com*

travel advice

ORGANISING A SAFARI

While you can plan a safari to most of the lodges featured by contacting them directly, it is often simpler to employ the services of a specialist safari tour operator to coordinate your visit. In selecting your destinations and lodges, you'll need to specify your preferred type of safari. Do you prefer rustic bushcamps to upmarket luxury lodges? Are balloon trips or camel rides on your list of dreams? And are you a dedicated birdwatcher or are you a first-time visitor who wants to see the big five? An experienced operator will tailor-make an itinerary to accommodate both your scope of interests and your budget.

Africa Geographic Expeditions is the travel arm of Africa Geographic, with extensive experience in creating itineraries in Kenya, Tanzania and Uganda. It also offers expeditions, led by experts, to these and other countries in Africa. For more information, tel. (+27-21) 762 2180, fax (+27-21) 762 2246, e-mail *info@africageographic.com* or go to *www.africageographicexpeditions.com*

kenya

When to go

Kenya has a tropical climate, with humid coastal areas and hot, dry inland regions. The rainfall periods are April to June and October to December. The annual wildlife migration between Serengeti National Park in Tanzania and the Masai Mara National Reserve in Kenya occurs between June and September.

Getting there

More than 30 international and African airlines service Nairobi's Jomo Kenyatta International Airport and Moi International Airport near Mombasa. If you're flying on to a more remote destination, book the connecting flights first as they are less frequent. Safari lodges often offer charter flights from the major airports. A departure tax is payable when leaving from Jomo Kenyatta on international flights.

Visas

South Africans intending to visit for up to 30 days do not need a visa. Many other nationals do require entry visas – for details, contact your local Kenyan High Commission or tour operator. Certain nationals are able to purchase visas on arrival in Kenya.

Money matters

US dollars can be used throughout Kenya. Travellers' cheques can be exchanged at banks around the country, at forex bureaux in Nairobi and at most large hotels. Credit cards are widely accepted, except in rural areas.

Medical matters

Malaria is endemic to most parts of the country; intending visitors should start taking anti-malarial tablets at least two weeks prior to their visit. Mosquito repellents should be used after dusk, and clothes should cover your body. Vaccinations against yellow fever are compulsory. Since rules concerning disease prevention change from time to time, you should check with your tour operator or doctor if other vaccinations are necessary. Drink bottled water.

Clothing

Light summer clothing can be worn year round, although a fleecy sweater is recommended for mornings and evenings, when temperatures are often low. On safari, wear clothes that blend into the environment. Good shoes and a hat are essential, as are long-sleeved shirts and trousers for the evenings.

Birding

Kenya has more than 1 000 bird species. To identify your sightings, consult Ian Sinclair and Peter Ryan's *Birds of Africa* (Struik Publishers, Cape Town).

Photography

Both the scenic beauty and quality of light in Kenya provide year-round photographic opportunities. When photographing people, first ask permission and be prepared to barter with either a promissory copy of the picture or hard cash. Don't photograph sensitive subjects, such as military installations or airports. Although batteries, film and memory cards are available, they may be hard to find, so take your own. Also take a card reader or storage device. Lodges provide 220- to 240-volt power with flat-pronged plugs. If necessary, take an adaptor.

Don't forget

Binoculars for game-viewing, sunblock, lip balm and a torch.

When to go

Tanzania has a tropical climate. The rainy season is from March to the beginning of May, with showers in November and December. April to June sees the annual wildebeest migration, while the drier seasons offer good chimp-viewing in the Mahale region and excellent game-viewing in Katavi.

Getting there

South African Airways and numerous other international airlines fly into Dar es Salaam, Zanzibar or Kilimanjaro (50 kilometres from Arusha). Shuttle air services with Air Tanzania or charter flights will transport visitors to lodges; shuttle bus services are also available. Tanzania has a good network of tarred and all-weather roads connecting major towns, while minor roads become impassable to all except 4x4 vehicles during the rainy season. Expect dust in the dry season. A departure tax of US$25 is charged when leaving Zanzibar Airport for international destinations.

Visas

Visas are required by all visitors to Tanzania. They are available from your local High Commission of Tanzania, or can be purchased on arrival in Tanzania, at a cost of US$50.

Money matters

The easiest foreign currency to exchange or use in Tanzania is US dollars, which are accepted by safari companies, for aeroplane fares and national park fees and at tourist hotels and lodges. Most stores, restaurants, bus, taxi, train and ferry companies will take local currency only. Travellers' cheques can be exchanged at banks or forex bureaux. Credit cards can be used only at major tourist destinations. It's best to take a credit card for emergency use only.

Medical matters

Yellow fever vaccinations are compulsory, while those for hepatitis A, typhoid, meningitis and tetanus are recommended. Malaria is endemic and anti-malaria tablets are highly recommended. Drink bottled water.

Clothing

Light summer clothing is generally sufficient, although cooler night-time and high-altitude temperatures may require extra layers. As Tanzania has a large Muslim community, the dress is modest in certain areas – women must cover their shoulders and knees. The dress code for men is more relaxed, but they must never travel bare-chested. Wear neutral colours when on safari.

Birding

Tanzania ranks as one of Africa's top birding destinations. To identify your sightings, consult Ian Sinclair and Peter Ryan's *Birds of Africa* (Struik Publishers, Cape Town).

Photography

Tanzania offers loads of photographic opportunities. Do not photograph the people without first asking permission, and avoid taking pictures of military installations and other sensitive areas. Film and memory cards may not be easily available away from the main centres, so take your own. Also take a card reader or storage device. Tanzania has 230-volt electricity, with both round-pinned and square-pinned plug sockets available. Take an adaptor, if in doubt.

Don't forget

Binoculars for game-viewing, sunblock, lip balm, a hat and a torch.

When to go

Although Uganda lies on the equator, the climate is warm rather than hot, with little variation between the seasons. It can become cool, especially in the higher areas. The wettest months are April, May, October and November, when travelling on unsurfaced roads may be difficult. The best times to visit are the dry, although hot period from December to February, and mid-June to mid-August.

Getting there

Entebbe International Airport, 40 kilometres from Kampala, is serviced by several international and African airlines. South African Airways flies to Uganda three times weekly from Johannesburg. A departure tax of US$30 to US$50 must be paid to leave Uganda on international flights. There are daily connections to and from Nairobi, and several reputable domestic companies offer charter flights. 4x4 vehicles may be required to travel in the national parks and rural areas during the rainy seasons.

Visas

Visas are required by all nationals and must be obtained from diplomatic and consular missions before departure. However, regulations may change, so check with the local authorities before leaving.

Money matters

US dollars, British pounds and Euros are accepted. Travellers' cheques can be exchanged at banks and forex bureaux at the airport and in Kampala. Credit cards are accepted in the main hotels and lodges, but not in outlying areas. Once on safari, only cash can be converted, with larger US dollar denominations earning a better rate of exchange.

Medical matters

Vaccinations against yellow fever are compulsory, and are recommended against typhoid, hepatitis A, meningitis and tetanus. Take anti-malaria tablets. Drink bottled water.

Clothing

Light summer clothing supplemented by a sweater or jacket should be sufficient at all times. Cotton clothing in neutral colours is recommended for safaris, as is a hat and comfortable shoes. Rain jackets are essential for the rainy season, as are waterproof gloves, shoes and ankle garters to prevent water entering the top of your boots. For gorilla trekking, you'll need stout boots, long trousers and a long-sleeved shirt. Do not wear army-style camouflage clothing.

Birding

Uganda's rich birdlife is attributable to its location at the confluence of the East African savanna, semi-desert to the north and West African rainforest. To identify your sightings, consult Ian Sinclair and Peter Ryan's *Birds of Africa* (Struik Publishers, Cape Town).

Photography

Photography is allowed in all areas apart from airports, military installations and other sensitive areas. Commercial photographers should consult the Ministry of Information for a permit. Bring your own batteries, film, memory cards, card reader and storage device. Uganda has 220-volt power and plugs with three flat prongs. Take an adaptor, if necessary.

Don't forget

Binoculars, sunblock, lip balm and a torch.

AFRICA
Geographic

An Africa Geographic publication
Africa Geographic
1st floor, Devonshire Court
20 Devonshire Road, Wynberg 7800
Cape Town, South Africa
www.africageographic.com

Reg. no. 1992/005883/07

First published 2006

Text & photographs © David Rogers and Ian Johnson
(with the exception of photographs individually credited)
Cover photograph of Mount Kilimanjaro © D. & S. Balfour/www.darylbalfour.com

Editor Judy Beyer
Art Director Bryony Branch
Travel and Lodge Coordinator Jenni Saunders

Reproduction in Cape Town by Resolution Colour (Pty) Ltd
Printed & bound by Tien Wah Press (Pte) Ltd, Singapore

ISBN 0 620 36514 5

AFRICA GEOGRAPHIC EXPEDITIONS

Further information on all the establishments featured in *East Africa – Safari in Style* can be
found at the end of each entry. Your local travel agent or consultant should also be able to
provide help and advice. You are also welcome to contact us at Africa Geographic Expeditions,
as we would be delighted to help you plan a visit to these properties or any other destination in
Africa. Africa Geographic Expeditions offers many superb itineraries designed for the readers of
Africa Geographic magazine. More about these can be found on our website.

Africa Geographic Expeditions
Devonshire Court
20 Devonshire Road
Wynberg 7700
Cape Town, South Africa
Tel. (+27-21) 762 2180
Fax (+27-21) 762 2246
E-mail *info@africageographic.com*
Website *www.africageographicexpeditions.com*